John Bell Hood
And the Struggle for Atlanta

CIVIL WAR CAMPAIGNS AND COMMANDERS SERIES

Under the General Editorship of Grady McWhiney

PUBLISHED

Battle in the Wilderness: Grant Meets Lee by Grady McWhiney
Death in September: The Antietam Campaign
    by Perry D. Jamieson
Texans in the Confederate Cavalry by Anne J. Bailey
Sam Bell Maxey and the Confederate Indians by John C. Waugh
The Saltville Massacre by Thomas D. Mays
General James Longstreet in the West: A Monumental Failure
    by Judith Lee Hallock
The Battle of the Crater by Jeff Kinard
Cottonclads! The Battle of Galveston and the Defense of the
    Texas Coast by Donald S. Frazier
A Deep, Steady Thunder: The Battle of Chickamauga
    by Steven E. Woodworth
The Texas Overland Expedition by Richard Lowe
Raphael Semmes and the Alabama by Spencer C. Tucker
War in the West: Pea Ridge and Prairie Grove by William L. Shea
Iron and Heavy Guns: Duel Between the Monitor and Merrimac
    by Gene A. Smith
The Emergence of Total War by Daniel E. Sutherland
John Bell Hood and the Struggle for Atlanta by David Coffey
The Most Promising Young Man of the South: James Johnston
    Pettigrew and His Men at Gettysburg by Clyde N. Wilson

John Bell Hood
And the Struggle for Atlanta

David Coffey

McWhiney Foundation Press
McMurry University
Abilene, Texas

Cataloging-in-Publication Data

Coffey, David A. (David Alan), 1960–
    John Bell Hood and the struggle for Atlanta / David A. Coffey.
        p. cm. — (Civil War campaigns and commanders series)
    Includes bibliographical references and index.
    ISBN-10: 1-886661-17-0
    ISBN-13: 978-1-886661-17-2

    1. Hood, John Bell, 1831–1879—Military leadership. 2. Atlanta
Campaign, 1864. 3. Generals—Confederate States of America—
Biography. 4. Confederate States of America. Army—Biography.
I. Title. II. Series.
        E476.1.H58C64 1998
        973.7'371'092—dc21   98–25133
                                                                          CIP

McMurry Station, Box 637
Abilene, TX 79697-0637

Printed in the United States of America

ISBN-10: 1-886661-17-0
ISBN-13: 978-1-886661-17-2
10 9 8 7 6 5 4 3 2

Book Designed by Rosenbohm Graphic Design

All inquiries regarding volume purchases of this book should be
addressed to McWhiney Foundation Press, McMurry Station, Box 637,
Abilene, TX 79697-0637.
Telephone inquiries may be made by calling (325) 572-3974

A NOTE ON THE SERIES

Few segments of America's past excite more interest than Civil War battles and leaders. This ongoing series of brief, lively, and authoritative books–*Civil War Campaigns and Commanders*–salutes this passion with inexpensive and accurate accounts that are readable in a sitting. Each volume, separate and complete in itself, nevertheless conveys the agony, glory, death, and wreckage that defined America's greatest tragedy.

In this series, designed for Civil War enthusiasts as well as the newly recruited, emphasis is on telling good stories. Photographs and biographical sketches enhance the narrative of each book, and maps depict events as they happened. Sound history is meshed with the dramatic in a format that is just lengthy enough to inform and yet satisfy.

Grady McWhiney
General Editor

In Memory Of
Jerry Coffey and Carole Humphrey Coffey
Fine Writers, Gifted Editors, and Wonderful Parents

CONTENTS

Introduction: Hood Is Not Dead   13

1. A Storm Suddenly Arose   21

2. The Joe Johnston Mode of Warfare   33

3. The Weight of Responsibiliy   48

4. The Lee and Jackson School   59

5. Brilliant But Disastrous   73

6. No Decided Advantage   87

7. Atlanta Is Ours   98

6. Conclusion: So Strangely Misrepresented   112

Appendix A.
Confederate Forces During the Atlanta Campaign   118

Appendix B.
Union Forces During the Atlanta Campaign   135

Bibliography   162

Index   167

CAMPAIGNS AND COMMANDERS SERIES

Map Key

Geography

 Trees

 Marsh

Fields

Strategic Elevations

Rivers

Tactical Elevations

 Fords

 Orchards

 Political Boundaries

Human Construction

 Bridges

 Railroads

 Tactical Towns

 Strategic Towns

Buildings

Church

Roads

Military

 Union Infantry

 Confederate Infantry

 Cavalry

 Artillery

Headquarters

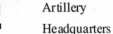 Encampments

 Fortifications

 Permanant Works

Hasty Works

Obstructions

 Engagements

 Warships

 Gunboats

 Casemate Ironclad

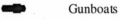 Monitor

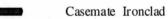 Tactical Movements

 Strategic Movements

*Maps by
Donald S. Frazier, Ph.D.
Abilene, Texas*

MAPS

The Atlanta Campaign   32

The Atlanta Vicinity   58

Peachtree Creek, July 20, 1864   68

The Battle of Atlanta, July 22, 1864   76

The Battle of Ezra Church, July 28, 1864   92

The Battle of Jonesboro, August 31, 1864   104

The Battle of Jonesboro, September 1, 1864   108

PHOTOGRAPHS AND ILLUSTRATIONS

John Bell Hood	14
Jefferson Davis	19
William T. Sherman	22
Joseph E. Johnston	24
Joseph Wheeler	28
George H. Thomas	34
James B. Mcpherson	36
John M. Schofield	38
Leonidas Polk	40
Jacob D. Cox	41
Patrick Cleburne	44
William J. Hardee	50
Braxton Bragg	52
Alexander P. Stewart	60
Benjamin Franklin Cheatham	62
Oliver O. Howard	64
Joseph Hooker	66
Francis P. Blair, Jr.	78
Arthur M. Manigault	81
John A. Logan	82
Stephen D. Lee	88
George Stoneman	90
Alfred Iverson	95
Hugh Judson Kilpatrick	101
Jefferson C. Davis	110

John Bell Hood
And the Struggle for Atlanta

INTRODUCTION
HOOD IS NOT DEAD

In late September 1863 reports of a great victory spread through the Confederate states. General Braxton Bragg's long-beleaguered Army of Tennessee had routed Federal forces in northwestern Georgia in a brutal contest that became known as the Battle of Chickamauga. And on that bloody battlefield another Southern general entered the Confederate pantheon, taking his place beside the martyred Stonewall Jackson—at least temporarily.

As his troops drove through the Federal line, Major General John Bell Hood fell desperately wounded. Throughout the Confederacy, word of Hood's heroic demise accompanied reports of Bragg's victory. "Hood," Confederate War Department clerk John B. Jones recorded, "is said to be dead." And, by the nature of his wound, he might well have been. A Yankee bullet struck the upper third of his right leg, shattering the bone, and necessitating the amputation of the limb. But Hood survived the dangerous operation and received the finest care available. Four days after the battle, Jones could report: "Hood is not dead, and will recover." Already a star on the rise, Hood now became a Southern hero, destined to take a leading role in the final stages of the war.

Born to a prosperous family at Owingsville, Kentucky, on June 29, 1831, John Bell Hood grew up in an environment steeped in romanticism and Southern aristocratic values. Although urged by his physician father to pursue a career in medicine, young Hood, as he recalled in his memoir, "fancied a military life." Through an uncle in Congress, he received an appointment to the United States Military Academy in 1849. At West Point he struggled with his studies, and a marked lack of discipline almost cost him his

JOHN BELL HOOD

Born Kentucky 1831; Hood was graduated from the U.S. Military Academy in 1853, forty-fourth in his class of fifty-two that included Philip Sheridan, James B. McPherson, and John M. Schofield; commissioned 2d lieutenant, he served on the frontier most notably with the elite 2d Cavalry, a regiment that included Robert E. Lee, Albert Sidney Johnston, William J. Hardee, George H. Thomas, and many other future Civil War generals; while on duty in Texas, Hood was wounded in an engagement with Comanches; he resigned his 1st lieutenant's commission in 1861 to enter Confederate service at the same grade; he rose quickly through the ranks to major, commanding all cavalry at Yorktown; in October 1861 Hood became colonel of the 4th Texas Infantry; promoted to brigadier general in March 1862, he commanded the Texas Brigade during the Peninsular Campaign and the Seven Days Battles, during which the brigade spearheaded the Confederate breakthrough at Gaines' Mill; Hood commanded a division at Second Manassas, again delivering a crushing attack, and at Sharpsburg appointment. His classmates included future Federal generals Philip Henry Sheridan, John M. Schofield, and James B. McPherson. McPherson, who graduated first in the class of 1853, often assisted Hood in his studies. But Hood's most important West Point association came in 1852, when Robert E. Lee became superintendent. Hood managed to graduate with his class in 1853, ranking forty-fourth out of fifty-two.

Hood's low standing dictated an infantry assignment. In February 1854 Brevet Second Lieutenant Hood reported for duty at Fort Jones, an isolated post in northern California. But the young subaltern longed for a posting in the mounted arm of the service. To that end, in 1855 he applied for a position in

(Antietam), where his division was sacrificed to buy time for Lee's army; promoted to major general, he led his division at Fredericksburg and at Gettysburg, where a wound rendered his left arm virtually useless; returning to duty, he commanded General James Longstreet's Corps in the Confederate breakthrough at Chickamauga but was again wounded, losing his right leg; promoted to lieutenant general in February 1864 (to rank from September 1863), he joined the Army of Tennessee in March; he directed a corps during the Atlanta Campaign until selected to replace General Joseph E. Johnston with the temporary rank of full general; he fought a series of battles around Atlanta but was forced to evacuate that city on September 1, 1864; leading his army into Tennessee, he fought a bloody battle at Franklin in November and was routed at Nashville the following month; relieved at his own request in January 1865, he surrendered at Natchez, Mississippi, in May; after the war he engaged in business in New Orleans, married, and fathered eleven children; General Hood died at New Orleans along with his wife and eldest daughter during the yellow fever epidemic in 1879. As a combat commander, Hood was unsurpassed; he ranks among the best brigade and division commanders in the war. While not ideally suited to corps or army command, he performed credibly during the Atlanta Campaign; the utter failure of his Tennessee Campaign severely tarnished an otherwise stellar career.

one of two newly constituted cavalry regiments, and sought the influence of a childhood friend, politician John C. Breckinridge, in helping to achieve his transfer. With the possible aid of Breckinridge, Hood received an appointment as second lieutenant in the new 2d Cavalry Regiment, then being organized at Jefferson Barracks in Missouri.

"Little indeed did I anticipate at that period the great theatre of life [into which] I was destined so soon to be thrown as an humble actor," Hood recalled. The 2d Cavalry was a special regiment, in which Hood found himself among the army's elite. Colonel Albert Sidney Johnston headed the unit, with Lieutenant Colonel Robert E. Lee and Majors William J. Hardee and George Thomas filling the field-grade positions. Other future Civil War generals assigned to the regiment included Edmund Kirby Smith, Earl Van Dorn, Fitzhugh Lee, George Stoneman, and Kenner Garrard. In all, sixteen of the regiment's officers became Civil War generals. In late 1855 Hood marched with the regiment to Texas, where he remained on duty until November 1860. In 1857 he led a scouting expedition, during which he was wounded in an engagement with Comanches. The following year he received promotion to first lieutenant. But while he enjoyed a leave of absence in 1861, the secession crisis came to a head.

With never a doubt as to which side he would follow, Hood resigned his United States Army commission in April 1861. Since Kentucky did not secede, he recalled, "I entered the Confederate service from the State of Texas, which thenceforth became my adopted land." As a newly commissioned first lieutenant, Hood then reported to Richmond, Virginia, where he received his first orders from his old mentor, Robert E. Lee. Hood thus began an incredible career that would take him to the highest echelons of his profession.

After directing the cavalry in the fighting at Yorktown, on the Virginia Peninsula, Hood was selected to head the 4th Texas Infantry Regiment. In March 1862 he received promotion to brigadier general to command a brigade that included three Texas regiments—thereafter known as Hood's Texas Brigade. Hood quickly turned his new command into one of the best brigades in Confederate service. He led his men during the Peninsular Campaign of spring 1862, and during the Seven Days' Battles in June. At Gaines' Mill, with Hood personally leading the 4th Texas, the brigade pierced the previously unbreakable Federal line, initiating a complete rout.

With Hood's military stock on the rise, Richmond society began to take notice. The diarist Mary Boykin Chesnut described "the famous colonel of the Fourth Texas" as having a "sad Quixote face, the face of an old crusader who believed in his cause, his cross, his crown—we were not prepared for that type exactly as a beau idéal of wild Texans." He possessed "an appearance of awkward strength," she continued, "tall—thin—shy," with blue eyes, blond hair, and a tawny beard. "Him we called Sam," wrote Mrs. Chesnut, "because his classmates at West Point did so still."

In polite society Hood appeared vulnerable, reserved, rough, and often woefully out of place. Not so on the battle-field, where he seemed most at home, where he excelled. "The man was transfigured," Captain Charles Venable of Lee's staff noted, "the fierce light of his eyes—I shall never forget."

Hood commanded a division in the July 1862 Second Manassas Campaign, and again delivered a crushing attack. Then, at Antietam, he sacrificed his division to save Lee's army. He had become a true standout in an already legendary army, and in October, at thirty-one years of age, he became one of the youngest major generals in the Confederate army. His troops were only lightly engaged at Fredericksburg in December, and missed altogether the great victory at Chancellorsville the following spring. Even so, the Texan had passed through some of the bloodiest days in American history unscathed, despite often being in the thick of the most heated action. But then came Gettysburg.

On July 2, 1863, during the second day of the great battle, Lieutenant General James Longstreet, on orders from General Lee, directed Hood to make a frontal attack on the most difficult portion of the enemy line—two small, wooded hills known as Big Round Top and Little Round Top. He requested permission from Longstreet to take his division around the exposed Federal flank to strike the unprotected rear. When Lee refused this request, Hood repeated it twice more with the same result. After registering a protest—"the first and only one" of his military career—he advanced his division as ordered. "In about twenty minutes," he remembered, "I was severely wounded in the arm, and borne from the field." Shell fragments tore through the general's left arm, doing serious nerve damage that left the limb virtually useless for the rest of his life. His division fought desperately only to be hurled back by the determined Federal resistance.

Little more than two months later, Hood's Division was dispatched to Georgia, along with most of Longstreet's Corps, to bolster General Braxton Bragg's beleaguered command. Though still not completely recovered, Hood went along. On September 20, during the final day of the Battle of Chickamauga, he directed a provisional corps that shattered the Federal line and propelled the Confederates to a stunning victory. And there he received the wound that required the amputation of his right leg just below the hip. He recovered gradually, and in mid-November he arrived at Richmond to a hero's welcome.

By December Hood was well enough to participate in Richmond society. He became a regular visitor to the Chesnut home, where he attempted to rekindle a rather one-sided romance with the beautiful Sally "Buck" Preston. According to Mrs. Chesnut, Buck "had a knack of being 'fallen in love with' at sight and of never being 'fallen out of love' with. But then, there seemed a spell upon her lovers—so many were killed or died of the effects of wounds." Indeed, since the time he had

JEFFERSON DAVIS

Born Kentucky 1808; attended Transylvania University; graduated U.S. Military Academy twenty-third in his class in 1828; appointed 2d lieutenant in the 1st Infantry in 1828; 1st lieutenant 1st Dragoons 1833; regimental adjutant 1833 to 1834; served on the Northwest frontier and in the Black Hawk War in 1832; resigned from the army in 1835 and eloped with Zachary Taylor's daughter, who died of malaria three months after their marriage; Davis settled in Mississippi as a planter; married Varina Howell and was elected to Congress in 1845; resigned to participate in the Mexican War; appointed colonel 1st Mississippi Volunteer Infantry in 1846; serving under Taylor, he was wounded at Buena Vista in 1847; declined appointment to brigadier general; elected senator from Mississippi in 1847; secretary of war under President Franklin Pierce from 1853 to 1857; returned to the Senate where he served on military affairs committee until his resignation in 1861; president of the

Confederate States of America from 1861 to 1865; captured following the war in Georgia, he was imprisoned at Fort Monroe for two years and never brought to trial; after failing in a number of business ventures, he was a poor man during his later years, living at "Beauvoir," a house on the Gulf of Mexico given to him by an admirer; Mississippi would have sent him to the Senate, but he refused to ask for the Federal pardon without which it was impossible for him to take his seat; published *The Rise and Fall of the Confederate Government* in 1881; died in New Orleans in 1889. A biographer called Davis "a very engaging young man, fearless, generous, modest, with personal charm, and in friendship rashly loyal." His loyalty to the Southern cause also never faltered. But as a president he proved to be prideful, stiff, stubborn, often narrow-minded, unwilling to compromise. These qualities kept him from becoming a great chief executive.

met Buck and "surrendered at first sight," Hood had taken two wounds, one of them life-threatening. Despite his considerable handicap, he continued to pursue Miss Preston.

Hood also became a frequent companion of President Jefferson Davis. By mid-January the Texan could again ride a horse, and he often accompanied Davis on rides about the city, during which they discussed military issues and the president's desire to promote the young hero. Among the topics addressed were plans to reinforce the Western army for an offensive to retake Tennessee, and Hood's possible role in such an endeavor. Hood's already high opinion of the president grew considerably during this period.

Both Longstreet and Bragg had recommended Hood's promotion to lieutenant general following the Battle of Chickamauga. Davis, too, favored the idea, but no opening existed. When D.H. Hill's appointment failed to pass the Senate, and Davis refused to resubmit Hill's name, a vacancy opened for Hood. Critics would claim that Hood pandered his way to promotion, but he had earned it on the battlefield and had paid a high price in doing so. He embodied everything Davis sought in a general and, with Lee's army fully staffed with corps commanders, Davis decided to send Hood to Georgia, where it was hoped Hood could provide offensive punch to the Western army.

On February 11, 1864 the Senate confirmed Hood's promotion to lieutenant general, and shortly thereafter he received orders to report to Dalton, Georgia, and assume a corps command in the Army of Tennessee. Hood also believed that he secured a promise of marriage from the elusive Buck Preston, although her parents vehemently objected. Before leaving Richmond he confided to Mrs. Chesnut, "this has been the happiest year of any, in spite of all my wounds."

1
A STORM SUDDENLY AROSE

As Hood prepared to leave Richmond for his new assignment with the Western army, not even he could have imagined the course his career was about to take. After receiving the accolades of an adoring public, enjoying the company of an admiring president, and basking in the glory of his promotion, Hood now embarked on a new phase. He had seen some of the war's fiercest fighting and paid a heavy price, but this had come easily—almost naturally—compared to what lay in store. As he lamented long afterward: "After a journey over a smooth sea for many days—aye three years—a storm suddenly arose which lasted not only to the close of the war, but a long period thereafter."

The storm began with the very event that brought Hood his greatest glory—the Battle of Chickamauga. What appeared to be a decisive Confederate victory became otherwise when the devastated Federal army escaped to fight again. "We await the sequel," wrote war clerk Jones, "with fear and trembling, after the sad experience of Western victories." Jones proved prophetic as little more than two months later many of the

WILLIAM T. SHERMAN

Born Ohio 1820; graduated from U.S. Military Academy 1840, sixth in his class; 2d lieutenant 3rd Artillery 1840; 1st lieutenant 1841; stationed in California during Mexican War; captain 1850. Resigned from army 1853 to become banker; after business failed, Sherman voluntarily assumed personal financial responsibility for money lost by his friends; practiced law for a short time in Kansas, losing only case he tried; from 1859 to 1861 superintendent of military college that later became Louisiana State University. Colonel 13th Infantry and then brigadier general volunteers 1861; commanded brigade at First Bull Run; commanded division at Shiloh; major general volunteers 1862 to 1864, serving under Grant in the Vicksburg and Chattanooga campaigns; brigadier general U.S. Army 1863; major general 1864; assumed direction of principal military operations in the West. Directed Meridian and Atlanta campaigns, March to the Sea, and Carolina campaign that ended in surrender of Joseph E. Johnston's army in 1865; received thanks of Congress "for gallant and arduous services" during the Civil War; lieutenant general 1866; general 1869; commander of the army 1869 to 1883; retired 1883; published memoirs 1875; died 1891. Made his famous statement, "war is all hell," in a speech at Columbus, Ohio, in 1880. An officer noted that Sherman's "features express determination, particularly the mouth. He is a very homely man, with a regular nest of wrinkles in his face, which play and twist as he eagerly talks on each subject; but his expression is pleasant and kindly." Some authorities rate him an even better general than Grant.

same men who fled before the onrushing Rebels at Chickamauga joined in the attack that drove General Bragg's Army of Tennessee from Missionary Ridge.

Despite major victories in 1863 at Gettysburg, Vicksburg, and Chattanooga, U.S. President Abraham Lincoln found that ultimate victory and the restoration of the Union remained beyond his grasp. The battlefield victories also did little to quiet increasingly vociferous calls for an end to the fighting. Public support for Lincoln's war initiative had dwindled to the point that his re-election appeared doubtful. Democratic opponents called for a negotiated peace and draft riots had erupted throughout the North.

But Lincoln's uncertain future only strengthened his resolve to use his remaining time in office to complete the task of returning the rebellious states to the Union. His appointment of Ulysses S. Grant as general in chief of the Armies of the United States—complete with the newly revived rank of lieutenant general in the Regular Army—attested to Lincoln's commitment to a total effort to win the war. In Grant, Lincoln believed he had found the man to lead the Federal army to victory.

Grant moved quickly to prepare for the coming spring campaigns. He envisioned a massive effort designed to capitalize on the North's substantial numerical and logistical advantages by isolating Rebel armies and preventing them from reinforcing each other. He planned a major thrust aimed at General Robert E. Lee's Army of Northern Virginia that guarded the Confederate capital at Richmond, Virginia, and the rail connections to the supply centers in the Deep South. Grant would personally direct this campaign. The other primary objective, General Joseph E. Johnston's Army of Tennessee, was entrusted to Grant's friend and long-time lieutenant, Major General William Tecumseh Sherman.

Sherman, on Grant's recommendation, assumed direction of the Military Division of the Mississippi, a massive command that included the Departments of the Cumberland, the Ohio, the Tennessee, and the Arkansas. In a letter dated April 4, 1864 Grant outlined for Sherman his master design, including Sherman's assignment:

> You I propose to move against Johnston's army, to break it up, and to get into the interior of the enemy's country as far as you can, inflicting all the damage you can against their war resources.

JOSEPH E. JOHNSTON

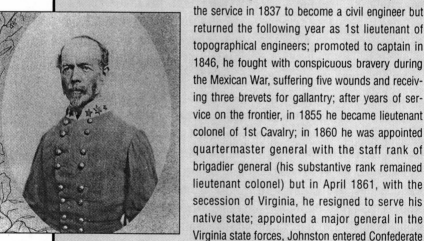

Born Virginia 1807; Johnston was graduated from the U.S. Military Academy in 1829, thirteenth in his class of forty-six; commissioned a 2d lieutenant of artillery, he served on the frontier and against the Seminoles in Florida; he left the service in 1837 to become a civil engineer but returned the following year as 1st lieutenant of topographical engineers; promoted to captain in 1846, he fought with conspicuous bravery during the Mexican War, suffering five wounds and receiving three brevets for gallantry; after years of service on the frontier, in 1855 he became lieutenant colonel of 1st Cavalry; in 1860 he was appointed quartermaster general with the staff rank of brigadier general (his substantive rank remained lieutenant colonel) but in April 1861, with the secession of Virginia, he resigned to serve his native state; appointed a major general in the Virginia state forces, Johnston entered Confederate service as a brigadier general in May 1861 and took command of the Harper's Ferry garrison; he led this force to Manassas Junction, where he became senior officer during the first major battle of the war; promoted to full general in July 1861, he was upset to find he ranked fourth among the Confederacy's generals (he believed that his staff rank in the U.S. Army dictated that he be first in seniority); this triggered a conflict with President Jefferson Davis that would last the rest of their lives; this notwitstanding, Johnston led the primary Rebel

> I do not propose to lay down for you a plan
> of campaign, but simply to lay down the work
> it is desirable to have done, and leave you free
> to execute in your own way.

Sherman now held the second most important position in the United States Army. His task, while symbolically less significant than Grant's, could, in real terms, if completed, yield more meaningful results. Sherman had long believed that the

army during the Peninsular Campaign of 1862 and had retreated to the outskirts of Richmond before he was wounded in the Battle of Seven Pines; General Robert E. Lee assumed command and fought a bloody campaign to save the capital; returning to duty, Johnston was ordered to take command of the Department of the West, a huge command that included all Confederate forces between the Appalachian Mountains and the Mississippi; he failed to mount a serious effort to relieve Federal pressure on Vicksburg in the summer of 1863; after the disaster at Missionary Ridge he replaced General Braxton Bragg as commander of the Army of Tennessee; during the early stages of the 1864 Atlanta Campaign, Johnston conducted a skillful strategic withdrawal that frustrated Davis, who wanted an offensive; after retreating to the vicinity of Atlanta, Johnston was relieved and replaced by General John B. Hood; recalled to duty by Lee in early 1865, Johnston opposed General W.T. Sherman in North Carolina before surrendering in April; following the war he engaged in numerous business activities, served in the U.S. House of Representatives from Virginia (1879-1881), and was a U.S. railroad commissioner (1885-1891); he devoted much of his time to defending his actions during the war and attacking Davis and Hood; to this end he published several articles and an extensive memoir, *Narrative of Military Operations* (1874); he died at Washington in 1891 of complications from a cold he reportedly contracted while attending Sherman's funeral. Immensely popular, Johnston enjoyed a splendid reputation, largely the result of his own writings; he was a gifted organizer and a master of the strategic withdrawal; but, while personally brave in the extreme, he was reluctant to risk offensive action.

war would be won in the West; this was his chance to prove his theory.

Following its devastating defeat at Chattanooga the previous November, the shattered Confederate Army of Tennessee withdrew into the mountains of northern Georgia to pass the winter. Its commander, Braxton Bragg, yielding to cries for his ouster, asked to be relieved. Senior corps commander Lieutenant General William J. Hardee headed the army temporarily but declined President Davis's offer of permanent command. In late December 1863 Davis reluctantly appointed General Joseph E. Johnston as Bragg's replacement.

Davis's relationship with Johnston was less than cordial. Johnston had been the senior officer on the field during the Confederate victory at First Manassas (Bull Run), and despite being the primary field commander in the East, he ranked fourth in seniority among the South's full generals. Johnston believed his place in the prewar U.S. Army (he had held the staff rank of brigadier general) dictated that he should be the Confederacy's top soldier. His open resentment toward Davis on this account had only intensified during subsequent disputes. During the Peninsular Campaign of 1862, Johnston defied Richmond authorities by pulling his army to within a few miles of the capital before he was wounded in the Battle of Seven Pines and replaced by Robert E. Lee. Following his return to duty, he was given an expansive theater command in the West, where he did little to aid the beleaguered garrison at Vicksburg. Davis, consequently, had little confidence in the fifty-seven-year-old general. Johnston's campaign of words against the president, often carried on through friends in the Confederate Congress, combined with his ineffectual field performance, did nothing to change Davis's opinion.

Regardless of Davis's feelings, the soldiers of the star-crossed army considered Johnston their savior and redeemer. Tennessee veteran Sam Watkins echoed the sentiments of many a soldier:

> Old Joe Johnston had taken command of the
> Army of Tennessee when it was crushed and
> broken, at a time when no other man on earth
> could have united it. He found it in rags and
> tatters, hungry and heart-broken, the morale of
> the men gone, their manhood vanished to the
> winds, their pride a thing of the past. Through
> his instrumentality and skillful manipulation,
> all these things had been restored.

But while Johnston did much to restore the condition of the army, he made little tactical preparation for the expected spring campaigns.

From the time of Johnston's appointment, Davis made clear his desire for an offensive campaign into Tennessee before the Federals could move on the vital states of Georgia and Alabama. But Johnston, claiming insufficient means for such an endeavor, offered no plan and rejected those proposed by Davis. For his part, Davis refused to commit additional forces without some assurance that Johnston would use them for offensive purposes. Without reinforcements and supplies that the Confederacy could not, or would not, provide, Johnston refused to take the initiative. As May brought the prospect of renewed fighting, Johnston seemed resigned to await a Union onslaught, which was precisely what Davis wished to avoid. Still, with Sherman's host massing in northern Georgia, Davis remained hopeful that Johnston would meet the advancing Federal army and defeat it quickly.

Johnston had inherited an army in desperate need of reorganization. Dismissals of senior commanders carried out by Bragg following the disaster at Missionary Ridge had stripped the Army of Tennessee, for better or worse, of much of its top brass. Its two infantry corps were commanded by Hardee and Thomas C. Hindman, who was only a major general, and the cavalry corps by youthful Major General Joseph Wheeler.

Neither Hindman nor Wheeler had much experience in directing a corps. Johnston petitioned Richmond for permission to organize his infantry into three corps as in Lee's Army of Northern Virginia. For this arrangement he requested Hindman's promotion and the appointment of an additional lieutenant general, suggesting several possible candidates. Failing that, he at least wanted an experienced officer for Hindman's corps. Richmond authorities denied these and other requests. Johnston would get a new lieutenant general, but he would be chosen by Davis.

Joseph Wheeler

Born Georgia 1836; Wheeler was graduated from the U.S. Military Academy in 1859, nineteenth in his class of twenty-two; commissioned a 2d lieutenant, he was posted to the 1st Dragoons but transferred to the Mounted Rifles; in March 1861 he entered Confederate service as a 1st lieutenant of artillery and

was on duty at Pensacola, Florida, before his resignation from the U.S. Army had been accepted; he was then elevated to colonel and given charge of the 19th Alabama Infantry, with which he served conspicuously at Shiloh; pegged as chief of cavalry for the Army of Mississippi (later Army of Tennessee) in July 1862, Wheeler fought numerous engagements during General Braxton Bragg's Kentucky Campaign; promoted to brigadier general in October, his performance in actions associated which the Battle of Murfreesboro earned him further promotion to major general in January 1863; Wheeler raided extensively throughout 1863 and participated in the Battle of Chickamauga and during the siege of Chattanooga; after accompanying General James Longstreet's command to Knoxville, he rejoined Bragg's army following its collapse at Missionary Ridge and assisted in the defense of Ringgold Gap that saved the Rebel army from total destruction; during the Atlanta

John Bell Hood was not among the names Johnston had submitted to Richmond, but Hood's selection appeared to please the general. Shortly after receiving word of the decision, Johnston wired Richmond: "Hood is much wanted here." Hood arrived at Dalton, Georgia, on February 25 and assumed command of his new corps three days later, superseding Hindman. Angered by the fact that a man junior to him in age and, until recently, rank had received the position to which he felt entitled, Hindman offered his resignation, but Davis refused to accept it. Hood quickly became a close confidant of

Campaign of 1864, Wheeler and his troopers performed tirelessly, especially in routing two major Federal raids and in providing excellent support of the infantry; but his August raid, in which he deviated from his instructions and moved into eastern Tennessee, almost destroyed his corps and left General John B. Hood in Atlanta without much needed reconnaissance; when Hood moved into Tennessee, Wheeler and most of his command remained in Georgia to oppose General W.T. Sherman's March to the Sea but his troops' lack of discipline earned them the wrath of Georgians and fellow Confederates alike; in 1865 he often fought successfully in the hopeless Carolina Campaign and fled with a portion of his command to Georgia prior to General J.E. Johnston's surrender; captured, he was imprisoned until June; after the war he settled in Alabama, where he became a planter; he also served eight terms in the U.S. House of Representatives; at the outbreak of the Spanish-American War, Wheeler offered his services and was commissioned a major general of volunteers; he led troops in Cuba and the Philippines and was commissioned a brigadier general in the regular army before his retirement in 1900; thereafter he lived in Brooklyn, New York, until his death in 1906. General Wheeler was undoubtedly a gifted cavalry commander; his aggressive style resulted in three wounds, sixteen mounds shot from beneath him, and the felling of thirty-six nearby staff officers; his command, however, was plagued by poor discipline, especially when operating away from the main army, and his raids frequently proved more detrimental to the Confederacy than to the Federals.

his new commander; he frequently dined with Johnston and often accompanied him on leisurely rides. Despite claims to the contrary, nothing in Hood's behavior upon joining the Army of Tennessee indicated a preexisting intention to undermine Johnston.

Within days of his arrival, Hood began what became a series of communications with Richmond. He may have been asked by Davis to update the government on conditions in Georgia, but, at least initially, his letters to Davis, Bragg (who now served as a military adviser to the president), and Secretary of War James Seddon supported Johnston's position. Hood wrote Davis on March 7: "I am exceedingly anxious, as I expressed to you before leaving Richmond, to have this Army strengthened, so as to enable us to move to the rear of the enemy and with a certainty of success. An addition of ten or fifteen thousands (10,000 or 15,000) men will allow us to advance." But as it became clear to Hood that Johnston did not intend to take the offensive, the tone and substance of his letters changed.

On April 13 Hood responded to a letter from Bragg: "I have done all in my power to induce General Johnston to accept the proposition you made to move forward. He will not consent. I regret this exceedingly," Hood continued, "as my heart was fixed upon going to the front, and regaining Tennessee and Kentucky." While it was patently inappropriate for subordinate commanders to communicate with the government over the head of the commanding general, Hood's comments were clearly solicited. Nor was Hood, contrary to later assertions, alone in this. Hardee, Wheeler, and division commander Major General Alexander P. Stewart also corresponded with Richmond—all voicing similar concerns.

His disappointment notwithstanding, Hood devoted himself during the months of March and April to preparing his corps for future campaigning—in whatever form it might take. He made a favorable impression on his new troops and, despite his abbreviated right leg, often rode up to fifteen miles in a day with little distress. Although he wore a cork leg complete with boot and spur, he relied on crutches to get around and had to be strapped to the saddle when riding. He had lost none of his handsome appearance or soldierly bearing. One observer noted that Hood "is a good officer [and] the finest looking man I think I ever saw."

As May approached, much to the chagrin of Richmond and many of his own officers, Johnston prepared to meet Sherman's advance. The army was experienced, rested, and, most important, well situated. The densely wooded mountainous terrain of northern Georgia appeared naturally defensible; it also offered prospects for surprise. But the men of the Army of Tennessee knew better than to take a naturally defensible area for granted—Missionary Ridge remained a vivid memory. The only questions that remained were: could Johnston repel the blue-clad invaders? Or, more important, would he try?

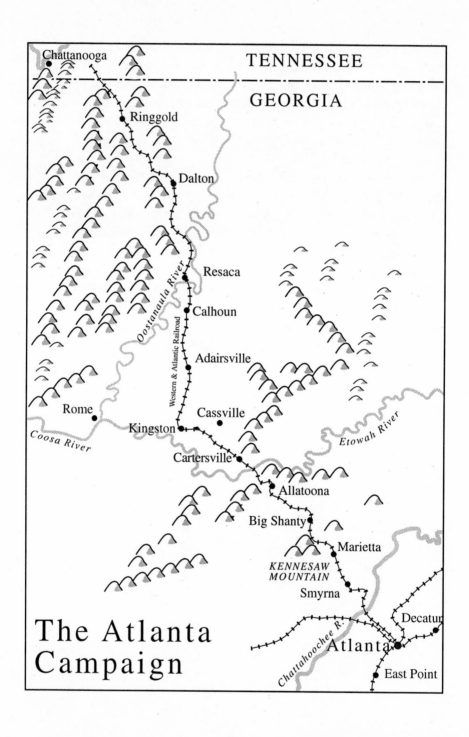

2
THE JOE JOHNSTON
MODE OF WARFARE

Hood derisively termed what he and his comrades experienced over the next two-and-a-half months the "Joe Johnston mode of warfare." There would be no advance into Tennessee—no offensive, and very little glory. "If I had had a conception of the operations from Dalton to Atlanta," Hood lamented years later, "naught but the most peremptory orders could have induced me to have left General Lee." Indeed, Johnston's approach proved far removed from that which Lee had employed so successfully during the previous two years, and General Sherman intended to take what was offered.

Sherman concentrated his forces near Chattanooga, in preparation for the proposed advance. His fighting force consisted of the Army of the Cumberland under Major General George H. Thomas, the Army of the Tennessee under Hood's former West Point classmate Major General James B. McPherson, and the smallish Army of the Ohio commanded by Major General John M. Schofield, another of Hood's former classmates. In all, Sherman had at his disposal more than 110,000 men in seven infantry corps and a cavalry corps, backed by more than 250 pieces of artillery. Although he stockpiled huge stores of supplies at Chattanooga, Sherman remained dependent on a tenuous rail link to Nashville and Louisville to fill the needs of his giant army, its animals, and the thousands of support personnel. As the appointed starting date of May 5 approached, Sherman stood poised to move on

GEORGE H. THOMAS

Born Virginia 1816; graduated U.S. Military Academy 1840, twelfth in his class of forty-two; assigned to artillery, he served on the frontier and in coastal defenses; he fought in the Seminole War and earned two brevets in the Mexican War; returning to West Point, he taught artillery and cavalry tactics; rising steadily through the ranks, Thomas became, in 1855, the junior major in the newly formed 2d Cavalry Regiment, an elite unit that included such future Civil War generals as A.S. Johnston, R.E. Lee, E. Kirby Smith, J.B. Hood, W.J. Hardee, Earl Van Dorn, and George Stoneman; serving on the Indian frontier and in Texas, Thomas made lieutenant colonel in April 1861 and was colonel when the 2d was redesignated the 5th Cavalry at the outbreak of the Civil War; although a Virginian, he remained loyal to the Union and was appointed brigadier general of U.S. Volunteers in August 1861; after serving briefly in the Shenandoah Valley, Thomas transferred to the Western Theater; he fought at Mill Springs, Kentucky, Shiloh, Corinth, and Perryville; promoted to major gen-

Joe Johnston's Confederate army positioned around Dalton, Georgia, just twenty miles to the southeast.

The Federal armies moved out of their camps as scheduled on May 5, 1864. Schofield's single corps, on the left, moved south from Red Clay on the Tennessee line via the East Tennessee & Georgia railroad. In the center, Thomas's 73,000-man Army of the Cumberland, advancing from Ringgold along the Western & Atlantic line, moved on Tunnel Hill. From the west, McPherson pushed his men toward Snake Creek Gap, hoping to gain the Confederate rear while Thomas and Schofield held the enemy near Dalton.

eral of volunteers in April 1862, he commanded a division at Stone's River; in September 1863 he commanded a corps during the Battle of Chickamauga, where he gathered the remnants of General W.S. Rosecrans's shattered force and held his ground long enough to prevent the army's total destruction; for this he earned the sobriquet "The Rock of Chickamauga"; promoted to brigadier general in the regular army in October 1863, he was given command of the Department and Army of the Cumberland; during the struggle for Chattanooga his command, acting without orders, drove the Confederates from Missionary Ridge; Thomas's Army of the Cumberland comprised more than half of General W. T. Sherman's force during the move on Atlanta in 1864, fighting steadfastly throughout that campaign; detached to oppose General J.B. Hood's strike into Tennessee, Thomas routed Hood at Nashville in December 1864; promoted to major general in the regular army shortly thereafter, he also received the thanks of Congress for Nashville; after the war he remained on duty in Tennessee before assuming command of the Department of the Pacific; General Thomas died at his headquarters in San Francisco in 1870. Although his slow, methodical approach often frustrated his superiors, Thomas was among the very best general officers to surface, on either side, during the war. Both Sherman and Grant downplayed Thomas's contribution to their success. That notwithstanding, his record reveals the important role he played in the Federal victory.

JAMES B. MCPHERSON

Born Ohio 1828; McPherson was graduated from the U.S. Military Academy in 1853, first in his class of fifty-two that included J.B. Hood, P.H. Sheridan, and J.M. Schofield; commissioned a 2d lieutenant of engineers, he taught at the academy and worked on coastal fortifications; promoted to 1st lieutenant in 1858 and captain in August 1861, he retained his staff assignment following the outbreak of the Civil War; promoted to lieutenant colonel in November 1861, he was aide-de-camp to General Henry Halleck in Missouri; he was General U.S. Grant's chief engineer during the battles at Forts Henry and Donelson, Shiloh, and in the advance on Corinth; promoted to colonel in May 1862, he entered the volunteer organization that same month as brigadier general; he commanded the Engineer Brigade, Army of the Tennessee, until his promotion to major general of volunteers in October 1862; he commanded the Seventeenth Corps, Army of the Tennessee, during the Vicksburg Campaign and was promoted to brigadier general in the regular army in August 1863; he led his corps in the Meridian Campaign and in March 1864 succeeded General W.T. Sherman as commander of the Department and Army of the Tennessee; he led the army, one of three in Sherman's conglomerate force, during the early stages of the Atlanta Campaign, but his indecisive actions at Snake Creek Gap in May and during the Battle of Peachtree Creek in July led to missed opportunities to crush the Confederate army; during the Battle of Atlanta in July 1864, General McPherson was killed by Rebel skirmishers as he rode unescorted to the scene of the fighting. A particular favorite of both Grant and Sherman, he was a loyal and dependable subordinate; as an army commander, however, he proved unequal to the responsibility.

Johnston positioned his army along the formidable Rocky Face Ridge protecting Dalton and the Western & Atlantic line. The aptly named ridge, cut by a series of gaps, was well suited for the defense. Along the ridge the corps of Hardee and Hood, roughly 47,000 strong, awaited the Federal advance, while Wheeler's 8,000 horsemen covered the flanks and numerous approaches. To improve the situation, Davis finally acceded to Johnston's call for men by ordering Lieutenant General Leonidas Polk with the bulk of his Army of Mississippi to reinforce the Army of Tennessee. Some fifteen miles to the south, two newly arrived brigades, the first of Polk's troops, protected the village of Resaca, where the Western & Atlantic crossed the Oostanaula River. But, through neglect or oversight, the narrow mountain passage, Snake Creek Gap, leading to Resaca and the Confederate rear, remained unprotected.

On May 7 the first shots of the campaign rang out as Thomas's advance drove Rebel outposts from Tunnel Hill, five miles northwest of Dalton. The following day Thomas closed on the main Confederate position on Rocky Face Ridge and heavy skirmishing ensued. As Thomas continued to press the issue along the ridge, advance elements of Schofield's Corps dueled with Wheeler's cavalry north of Dalton.

Although the action around Dalton featured some heated contact, Sherman had no intention of launching an all-out assault against the strongly held position. As planned, Thomas and Schofield were to hold Johnston in place while McPherson moved to cut the Rebel line of retreat.

On May 9 McPherson appeared well on the way to completing his mission. The hard-marching Army of the Tennessee moved through Snake Creek Gap with no resistance. Emerging from the gap, the Federals dispatched a single Rebel cavalry brigade and by mid-afternoon McPherson's entire army stood within five miles of Resaca. But unsure of his enemy's strength, McPherson declined to attack and withdrew to the mouth of the gap.

Only two Confederate infantry brigades and the remnants of the previously encountered cavalry—numbering, in all, no more than 4,000—had stood between McPherson's 25,000 veterans and Resaca. The opportunity to isolate Johnston and gain a quick victory vanished. Sherman cited timidity on McPherson's part for the failure; but, while McPherson's caution had lost for Sherman the chance for a spectacular victory, his capture of Snake Creek Gap achieved a positive result—he had flanked Johnston.

JOHN M. SCHOFIELD

Born New York 1831; Schofield was graduated from the U.S. Military Academy in 1853, seventh in his class of fifty-two that included John B. Hood, Philip H. Sheridan, and James B. McPherson; commissioned 2d lieutenant and assigned to artillery, he served on garrison duty in Florida and taught at West Point; promoted to 1st lieutenant, he took a leave of absence to teach physics at Washington University in St. Louis; he was promoted to captain, 1st Artillery, in 1861, and entered the Civil War as a major in the 1st Missouri Infantry, a regiment he later reorganized as the 1st Missouri Light Artillery; he served on the staff of General Nathaniel Lyon during the capture of Camp Jackson and in the Battle of Wilson's Creek, for which he earned the Medal of Honor; promoted to brigadier general, U.S. Volunteers in November 1861, he commanded the District of St. Louis and the Missouri Militia; after a succession of district commands, he was appointed major general, U.S.V., in November 1862, and commanded the Army of the Frontier until March 1863, when his appointment to major general lapsed for lack of Senate confirmation; he briefly headed a division in the Army of the Cumberland, but in May 1863 was reappointed and confirmed as major general to rank from November 1862; he commanded the Department of Missouri until February 1864, when he assumed command of the Department

Johnston escaped disaster, but he bore the responsibility for the error that left the door to his rear unprotected. And although the immediate threat had passed, McPherson's occupation of Snake Creek Gap rendered Johnston's position at Dalton untenable; the potential for catastrophe remained. On the night of May 12, Johnston withdrew his entire force from the Dalton area, leaving a position carefully prepared over the past six months. As Federal General Jacob Cox later observed, "the enemy had been compelled to evacuate the impregnable lines

and Army of Ohio; he led his army, the Twenty-third Corps, throughout General William T. Sherman's Atlanta Campaign; after that city's fall, Schofield was dispatched to oppose Hood's invasion of Tennessee; after escaping disaster at Spring Hill, he fought Hood at Franklin in November 1864; although not victorious, his force severely mauled the Confederates; he then led the Twenty-third Corps under General George H. Thomas in the rout of Hood's army at Nashville; elevated directly from captain to brigadier general in the regular army for his efforts in Tennessee, Schofield moved with his corps to North Carolina to participate in Sherman's final offensive; at the close of the war he was in command of the Department of North Carolina; brevetted major general, U.S.A., he was sent to France to negotiate an end to the French intervention in Mexico; continuing in the regular army, he served as Secretary of War from 1868 to 1869, during which time he recommended the acquisition of Pearl Harbor as a naval base; returning to active duty following the inauguration of U.S. Grant in 1869, he was elevated to major general; he served as superintendent of West Point from 1876 to 1881, and presided in the Fitz John Porter case; in 1888 he succeeded Sheridan as commanding general of the army; promoted to lieutenant general in 1895, he was retired later that year by operation of the law on his sixty-fourth birthday; General Schofield died at St. Augustine, Florida, in 1906. Despite his relative lack of combat experience, Schofield performed credibly in the latter stages of the war; the fact that he did so under Sherman's command largely accounted for his promotion over several more senior and, arguably, more deserving officers; throughout his post-war career, Schofield was a tireless advocate of military reforms.

LEONIDAS POLK

Born North Carolina 1806; attended the University of North Carolina and then the U.S. Military Academy, graduating eighth in his class of thirty-eight in 1827; brevetted 2d lieutenant and posted to artillery, Polk served only a few months before resigning to study for the Episcopal ministry; ordained a deacon in 1830, he became Missionary Bishop of the Southwest in 1838 and Bishop of Louisiana in 1841; assisted in the establishment of the University of the South at Sewanee, Tennessee; at the outbreak of the Civil War, Polk accepted a major general's commission from his close friend Confederate President Jefferson Davis; Polk's departmental command consisted of parts of Arkansas and western Tennessee; he committed a disastrous error in violating Kentucky's neutrality by occupying Columbus in September 1861, opening that state to Federal invasion; commanded a corps with gallantry but little skill at Shiloh and in the invasion of Kentucky; promoted to lieutenant general in October 1862, he directed a corps at Murfreesboro and a wing at Chickamauga; his overt criticism of General Braxton Bragg resulted in his banishment from the Army of Tennessee; he was given command of the Department of Alabama, Mississippi, and East Louisiana where he remained until ordered, in May 1864, to join the Army of Tennessee, now headed by Bragg's replacement General J.E. Johnston; Polk led his army (in effect, a corps) during the opening stages of the Atlanta Campaign; on June 14, 1864 he was instantly killed when struck by a solid shot while surveying Federal positions from Pine Mountain near Marietta, Georgia. General Polk's impact on the Confederate cause was largely negative. His violation of Kentucky neutrality proved irreparable and his feud with Bragg severely damaged the effectiveness of the Army of Tennessee. Davis's reluctance to remove Polk only exacerbated the situation.

JACOB D. COX

Born Canada 1828; graduated from Oberlin College in 1851, Cox practiced law in Ohio; a staunch abolitionist, he won election to the state senate in 1858; with the outbreak of the Civil War he was appointed a brigadier general of Ohio state troops and was soon commissioned at the same grade into the U.S. Volunteers; he served in western Virginia under General George B. McClellan and led a division at South Mountain; at Antietam in September 1862 he commanded the Ninth Corps; promoted to major general of volunteers in October, he served again in western Virginia and in April 1863 assumed command of the District of Ohio;

his major generalcy expired for lack of confirmation due to an overage at that grade and he reverted to brigadier; during the Atlanta Campaign of 1864, Cox commanded a division in General John M. Schofield's Twenty-third Corps, Army of the Ohio, and performed well throughout the campaign; detached to oppose General John B. Hood's Tennessee invasion, he performed conspicuously at Franklin and Nashville; reappointed and confirmed as major general in December 1864, he was then sent to North Carolina, where he headed a corps in the closing actions of the war; after the war he was elected governor of Ohio but his support for President Andrew Johnson's reconstruction program cost him his reelection in 1867; he served for two years as secretary of the interior in President U.S. Grant's administration; returning to his legal practice in 1870, he became president of the Wabash Railroad in 1873 and was elected to one term in the U.S. House of Representatives in 1876; always known for his intellect, Cox wrote extensively on the Civil War, including *Atlanta*, which was for many years the definitive work on that campaign; General Cox died at Gloucester, Massachusetts in 1900. Although recognized more as an author, he was a capable field commander in the later stages of the war.

about Dalton with but a trifling loss on the part of Sherman."

Hood was quite active during the first week of the campaign, and Johnston had relied extensively on his young corps commander. He dispatched Hood, not Hardee, to take charge when the emergency developed in the Confederate rear. Indeed, Hood quickly became Johnston's chief subordinate. He even found time to be baptized, prevailing upon the newly arrived Polk, who in addition to being a Confederate general was an Episcopal bishop, to perform the service.

After its well-conducted withdrawal the Army of Tennessee moved into prepared works at Resaca, where it found welcome reinforcement in the balance of Polk's command. The arrival of the Army of Mississippi gave Johnston some 18,000 additional troops, and Polk's three infantry divisions (roughly 14,000 men) became, in effect, a third corps. The bishop-general also brought Brigadier General William H. "Red" Jackson's excellent cavalry division that he placed at Johnston's disposal. Johnston now had more than 70,000 men—a large army by Confederate standards and the largest force Johnston could expect to get.

Sherman wasted no time in moving on Resaca. On May 14 skirmishing erupted along the four-mile front. Largely disorganized Federal advances were beaten back by elements of Hood's Corps. Late in the day, a counterattack by two divisions of Hood's Corps struck the exposed left flank of the Federal army, but reinforcements arrived to halt the Rebel attack.

While the fighting continued north of Resaca, a Federal division worked to cross the Oostanaula River to the west. Again Sherman threatened Johnston's flank. Sharp fighting continued the next day with Hood again heavily engaged, but Johnston, aware of the danger to his flank and rear, canceled Hood's planned afternoon attack and ordered another withdrawal. That night, the Army of Tennessee crossed the Oostanaula, following the Western & Atlantic in the direction of Calhoun, less than ten miles to the south.

A clear pattern had emerged. In one week, by employing strong turning movements, Sherman had forced Johnston out of two excellent positions without a major battle and with only light losses. Johnston, too, had avoided a large-scale engagement, opting to retreat rather than confront the Yankee challenge. The Confederate retreats had been well organized and skillfully conducted, but they were still retreats.

Finding Calhoun and then Adairsville unsuitable, Johnston fell back on Cassville, some twenty miles southeast of Resaca. In less than two weeks, he had retreated almost forty miles without attempting a major battle, but Cassville represented an opportunity to reverse the trend. Johnston planned for Hardee and Polk to block the paths of McPherson and Thomas, while Hood pounced on Schofield's undersized army. But before Hood could spring the trap on May 19, Federal cavalry advancing from the east diverted his attention. He could not attack as ordered without exposing his corps to attack from a Federal force of undetermined size. With the opportunity lost, Johnston had little choice but to pull his army into line at Cassville.

Johnston wanted to hold at Cassville; he disputed the assertions of Hood and Polk, who believed their positions too vulnerable to stand under Federal fire. Johnston later maintained that his two corps commanders strongly urged the further withdrawal that began at midnight. Hood, however, insisted that "the recommendation" was "throughout the discussion coupled with the proviso: if [Johnston] did not intend to force a pitched battle." Hardee also wanted to stay and fight but Johnston opted to retreat.

South of the Etowah River, fifteen miles from Cassville, the Rebels established a strong line near Allatoona Pass—a rugged, forbidding area superbly situated for defense. Sherman closed rapidly, but finding Johnston's position too strong to risk attacking, he returned to the maneuver that had proved so effective.

PATRICK CLEBURNE

Born Ireland 1828; served for three years in the British Army before pur-
chasing his discharge and migrating to the United States in 1849; settling
in Helena, Arkansas, he became a naturalized citizen; worked as a druggist
and studied law, gaining admittance to the bar in 1856; in 1860 he helped
organize a local militia company, the Yell Rifles, and became its captain;

with the secession of Arkansas, Cleburne was
elected colonel of a regiment that eventually
became the 15th Arkansas; joined General
William J. Hardee's command in the advance
on Bowling Green, Kentucky, beginning a long
association and friendship with that officer;
promoted to brigadier general in March 1862,
Cleburne led a brigade with conspicuous skill at
Shiloh; commanding a provisional division, he
was instrumental in the Confederate victory at
Richmond, Kentucky, where he was shot
through the face; back with his brigade, he was
again wounded at Perryville in October 1862;
promoted to major general in December 1862,
he led a division at Murfreesboro and
Chickamauga; his command held its position
on Missionary Ridge during the rout of General Braxton Bragg's Army of
Tennessee and then covered Bragg's retreat; his stand at Ringgold Gap
may have saved the army from destruction; his off-the-battlefield actions,
however, cost him further promotion; he was an ardent member of the
anti-Bragg faction calling for that general's removal and his proposal to
arm slaves for service in the Confederate Army angered many, including
President Jefferson Davis; Cleburne fought throughout the Atlanta
Campaign, but was continually passed over for promotion; he was killed
during the savage fighting at Franklin, Tennessee, in November 1864.
General Cleburne was arguably the finest general officer in the Army of
Tennessee and among the best to emerge during the war. He was one of
only two foreign-born officers to become a major general in the
Confederate Army.

Temporarily abandoning his sole source of supply, the Western & Atlantic, Sherman ordered a broad sweep to the west of the Rebel position by his entire force that would compel Johnston to abandon Allatoona Pass. This time, Johnston moved to meet the Federal threat. Ranging some fifteen miles to the southwest of Allatoona, Hood's Confederates met the Federal Twentieth Corps in a serious clash on May 25. Outnumbered four-to-one but bolstered by canister fire from his massed artillery, Hood repulsed repeated assaults, inflicting 1,600 casualties to his own 300. The intensity of the fight prompted Federal soldiers to call the battle site the "Hell Hole." On any other day, the rural crossroad served as the home of New Hope Church.

Two days later, a portion of Federal Fourth Corps attacked the Confederate right, east of New Hope Church, at Pickett's Mill. The Yankees, though, ran into Major General Patrick Cleburne's excellent division from Hardee's Corps, which was temporarily under Hood's direction. Cleburne's veterans mauled the attackers. The intrepid Cleburne then launched a furious counterattack that ended the action. The Federals suffered 1,500 casualties to Cleburne's 500. Hood called this clash the "most brilliant affair of the whole campaign."

Johnston's actions, with Hood's men doing the bulk of the fighting, had effectively blocked Sherman's intended envelopment. Moreover, he had held the Federals in a precarious position for almost two weeks. After an inconsequential battle at Dallas, Sherman disengaged and returned to his railroad lifeline. Johnston opted not to contest the move. Thus, by the end of the first week of June, Sherman's host was safely astride the Western & Atlantic and in possession of Allatoona Pass and the town of Acworth. Johnston withdrew into the fastness of the nearby mountains to await Sherman's next move.

Fighting resumed in mid June, and Federal pressure all along his line induced Johnston to abandon yet another position. The Confederates then established a line centered on Kennesaw Mountain, just two miles behind the previous one. Fighting soon erupted on the new front, as Sherman again pressed the issue.

Acting on his own authority, Hood on June 22 launched a furious assault at Kolb's Farm. The Federals repulsed the effort, inflicting about 1,000 casualties. Although ill-advised, the intensity of Hood's attack made an impression on Federal commanders, who urgently summoned reinforcements. Even General Cox, no admirer of Hood, noted "the good generalship of the effort." Thereafter Sherman quickly closed on the Confederate lines.

On June 27 Sherman strangely chose to deviate from his previously successful policy of maneuver in favor of a general assault. Whether impatient or mistaken as to the strength of his enemy's position, Sherman ordered a frontal attack on the Rebel center at Kennesaw Mountain. The Federals suffered almost 3000 casualties in the futile effort.

Sherman promptly returned to his proven method of maneuver, sending McPherson to turn Johnston from his seemingly impregnable position. On July 2, with McPherson threatening his left flank, Johnston abandoned the Kennesaw line, falling back first on Smyrna, and then into a complex system of works north of the Chattahoochee River. The plan behind the elaborate system of forts and obstructions was to allow them to be held by a small force so that the bulk of the army could be freed for offensive action. The forts never came into play.

On July 8, as Federal troops began crossing the river, rather than meeting the threat with force, Johnston ordered yet another retreat. The next night, Johnston's army crossed the Chattahoochee and established a new line south of Peachtree Creek, less than ten miles north of downtown Atlanta.

For days, the church spires of Atlanta could be seen from Federal positions as the rugged mountains gave way to more manageable terrain. "Mine eyes have beheld the promised land," wrote Major James A. Connolly of the 123d Illinois Mounted Infantry to his wife. "The domes and minarets and spires of Atlanta are glittering in the sunlight before us, and only 8 miles distant." This served to strengthen Sherman's resolve and quicken the advance. Major Connolly observed Sherman "stepping nervously about, his eyes sparkling and his face aglow—casting a single glance at Atlanta."

During two months of almost ceaseless campaigning, counting desertions, casualties, and other causes, Johnston had lost 20,000 men, yet during his one-hundred-mile-long retrograde he had not once employed his entire force in a general battle. Sherman's losses were roughly the same, but he had started with almost twice Johnston's number. He had avoided a general battle as well, but this caution (especially that of McPherson) may have also prevented him from routing the Rebel army.

The last substantial natural obstacle between Sherman and his prize had been surrendered without a fight. The Federals began posturing for what they believed would be the final push on Atlanta. With his back to the city, Johnston would have to give battle, abandon the place, or stand a siege—but his time was running short.

3
THE WEIGHT
OF RESPONSIBILITY

From the Confederate capital at Richmond, President Jefferson Davis followed Johnston's retrograde with mounting anxiety. Johnston's repeated calls for reinforcements and cavalry raids on Sherman's communications only exacerbated the president's frustration. The Confederacy had sent Johnston all the help it could afford to send.

On July 10 Davis received a Johnston telegram that announced the Federal crossing of the Chattahoochee and his further withdrawal. If Johnston intended to hold Atlanta, he gave no indication. And if Johnston would not make a stand, he had to be removed. Atlanta would not be yielded without a fight.

Even before the decision to relieve Johnston was made, Davis grappled with the question of a successor. The problem was a lack of qualified candidates. General P.G.T. Beauregard held the requisite rank and may have been considered, but his relationship with Davis was, if possible, worse than Johnston's. Edmund Kirby Smith, the commander in the Trans-Mississippi, also held the rank of full general, but had done nothing to distinguish himself. The other full general available was Bragg, who had left the same army in disgrace less than seven months before. For Davis, the list of candidates likely consisted of only two names—Hardee and Hood.

Hood was, of course, known to Davis, who had grown fond of him during the time they had spent together while Hood recuperated in Richmond. He was clearly a fighter, as demonstrated by his unsurpassed combat record with Lee's Army of Northern Virginia and in actions under his command during the retreat to Atlanta. In letters to both Davis and Bragg, Hood had voiced his concern over Johnston's conduct of the campaign and emphasized his own eagerness to give battle.

On July 12 Davis, anticipating the eventuality, consulted Robert E. Lee: "What think you of Hood for the post?"

Lee's opinion was not altogether favorable. He replied by telegram: "Hood is a bold fighter. I am doubtful as to the other qualities necessary." The general then elaborated in a letter to Davis: "Hood is a bold fighter, very industrious on the battlefield, careless off, & I have had no opportunity of judging his action, when the whole responsibility rested upon him. I have a very high opinion of his gallantry, earnestness & zeal. Genl Hardee has more experience in managing an army." Davis faced a difficult decision between the experience of Hardee and the proven aggressiveness of Hood.

Hardee, in fact, had much to recommend him. He ranked as one of the Confederacy's most experienced corps commanders. Known and respected throughout the Army of Tennessee, "Old Reliable" had fought in most of that army's battles. Before the war, he had authored an important text on infantry tactics, served as commandant of cadets at West Point, and held a lieutenant colonelcy in the old 2d Cavalry—a regiment that also included Hood. He was sixteen years older than Hood, and two years his senior in rank. Hardee was also a Georgian; he would be fighting for his home.

But Hardee had rejected the command of the Army of Tennessee less than a year before, and Davis took this as a fear of responsibility. Finally, and most damaging to Hardee's case, was the pivotal role that Bragg was to play in the selection process. Hardee had been an outspoken critic of the former commander, and Bragg had not forgotten.

Davis, despite his personal dislike of Johnston, was reluctant to remove the still popular commander. In order to find out what, if anything, Johnston planned to do, he dispatched

WILLIAM J. HARDEE

Born Georgia 1815; Hardee was graduated from the U.S. Military Academy in 1838, twenty-sixth in his class of forty-five; commissioned into the 2d Dragoons, he served in Florida and was promoted to 1st lieutenant in 1839; he studied at the Royal Cavalry School at Saumur, France, returning to the U.S. in 1842; promoted to captain in 1844, he was captured early in the Mexican War but returned to duty and earned two brevets; afterward, he taught cavalry tactics at West Point and served on the frontier; his *Rifle and Light Infantry Tactics*, published in 1855, became the Army's standard training manual for years to come; also that year he was promoted to major in the newly formed 2d Cavalry Regiment, an elite unit that included Albert Sidney Johnston, Robert E. Lee, George Thomas, E. Kirby Smith, Earl Van Dorn, and John B. Hood among several other future Civil War generals; after service in Texas, Hardee became commandant of cadets at West Point; he was promoted to lieutenant colonel in 1860, but

General Bragg to Atlanta. Davis did not need to wait for Bragg's report for his worst fears to be confirmed. On July 11 Johnston wired Richmond: "I strongly recommend the distribution of the U.S. prisoners, now at Andersonville, immediately."

On July 13 Bragg arrived at Atlanta and wired Davis: "Our army all south of the Chattahoochee, and indications seem to favor an entire evacuation of this place." Davis responded the next day in a curious telegram that appeared to authorize Bragg to remove Johnston and replace him with Hardee. To this, Bragg telegraphed Davis on the fifteenth, "I am decidedly opposed, as it would perpetuate the past and present policy which he has advised and now sustains." If Bragg was indeed

resigned in January 1861 after Georgia's secession from the Union; he soon entered Confederate service as a colonel and was elevated to brigadier general in June 1861; after organizing troops in Arkansas, he led them to Kentucky; promoted to major general in October 1861, he commanded a corps at Shiloh the following April; thereafter most of his service was with the Army of Tennessee; promoted to lieutenant general in October 1862, he led his corps with great skill at Perryville, Murfreesboro, and Chattanooga, where his stand at Missionary Ridge helped save the army from total destruction; following General Braxton Bragg's removal in December 1863, Hardee temporarily headed the army but declined the permanent command; during the 1864 Atlanta Campaign, he openly resented Hood's promotion to command the Army, and performed inconsistently; after Atlanta's fall he was reassigned at his own request and commanded troops in opposition to General W.T. Sherman's March to the Sea and in the Carolinas; he surrendered with General J.E. Johnston in April 1865; after the war he settled at Selma, Alabama, where he engaged in planting and various other enterprises; he died at Wytheville, Virginia, in 1873. Known as "Old Reliable," General Hardee was among the Confederacy's most experienced and competent corps commanders; his inability to get along with Bragg and Hood, however, proved quite detrimental.

referring to Hardee, he had misled the president. In fact, at Cassville Hardee had urged Johnston to stand and fight and he, like Hood, had been discouraged by the long retreat. Perhaps Bragg chose this time to exact revenge for Hardee's past criticism, but the idea that Hardee favored withdrawal likely came from Hood.

BRAXTON BRAGG

Born North Carolina 1817; graduated U.S. Military Academy fifth in the 1837 class of fifty; appointed 2d lieutenant 3rd Artillery; promoted to 1st lieutenant in 1838 and to captain in 1846; participated in the Seminole War and won three

brevet promotions for gallant conduct during the Mexican War; in 1849 married Eliza Brooks Ellis, daughter of a Louisiana sugar cane planter; after routine garrison duty on the frontier, he resigned his brevet lieutenant colonelcy in 1856 to become a Louisiana sugar planter; in 1861 appointed Confederate brigadier general and assigned to Pensacola, Florida, where he changed the volunteers he found there into drilled and disciplined soldiers; promoted to major general and assigned command of the Gulf Coast from Pensacola to Mobile; in 1862 he received orders to move his troops by rail to join General A. S. Johnston's army at Corinth, Mississippi, for the Battle of Shiloh, during which Bragg served as army chief of staff and commanded a corps; after Johnston's death, upon the recommendation of his successor, General P.G.T. Beauregard, Bragg was promoted to full general; in June he in turn replaced General Beauregard when that officer took an unauthorized sick leave; deciding to invade Kentucky, Bragg moved the bulk of his army from Tupelo, Mississippi, to Chattanooga, Tennessee, by rail, and then joined General E. Kirby Smith in a

In a letter to Bragg on the fourteenth, Hood cited the failure to bring Sherman to battle, the loss of 20,000 men, and the need for reinforcements. But he also seemed to be making a case for himself, should Davis replace Johnston:

> I have, general, so often urged that we should force the enemy to give us battle as to almost be regarded reckless by the officers of

bold invasion of Kentucky; checked at Perryville in October by General D.C. Buell, Bragg retreated to Murfreesboro, Tennessee, where he fought a bloody battle against General W.S. Rosecrans in late 1862 and early 1863; Rosecrans's Tullahoma Campaign in June 1863 compelled Bragg to abandon Tennessee, but after receiving General James Longstreet's Corps from Virginia in September as reinforcements for the Battle of Chickamauga, he drove the Federals back into Chattanooga and began a siege that lasted until General U.S. Grant arrived from Mississippi in November 1863 and drove the Confederates back into Georgia; relieved of command of the Army of Tennessee, Bragg became President Davis's military adviser in February 1864; he exercised considerable power and served the president and the Confederacy well during the eight months he held this position, but his appointment came too late in the war for him to have a determinative impact; in January 1865, while still serving as the president's military adviser, Bragg engaged in his most ineffective performance as a field commander: he failed to prevent the Federals from taking Fort Fisher, which protected Wilmington, North Carolina, the last Confederate port open to blockade runners; Bragg spent the last weeks of the war under the command of General J.E. Johnston attempting to check General W.T. Sherman's advance; Bragg and his wife were part of the Confederate flight from Richmond until their capture in Georgia; Bragg, who lived in relative poverty after the war, died in Galveston, Texas, in 1876, and is buried in Mobile. Never a great field commander, he had talents the Confederacy needed but seldom used: the army possessed no better disciplinarian or drillmaster; an able organizer and administrator, he excelled as an inspector, possessed a good eye for strategy, and proved himself a dedicated patriot.

> high rank in this army, since their views have
> been so directly opposite. I regard it as a great
> misfortune to our country that we failed to give
> battle to the enemy many miles north of our
> present position. Please say to the President
> that I shall continue to do my duty cheerfully
> and faithfully, and strive to do what I think is
> best for our country, as my constant prayer is
> for our success.

Hood was a patriot and no doubt realized the urgency of the moment—something had to be done to save Atlanta. Still, he was less than honest in presenting his own case and in implying that Hardee favored Johnston's policy.

Honest or not, Hood's letter had the desired effect. On the fifteenth Bragg drafted a lengthy letter to Davis in which he provided a detailed accounting of his observations and evaluations. He ended by advising the president: "If any change is made Lieutenant-General Hood would give unlimited satisfaction, and my estimate of him, always high, has been raised by his conduct in this campaign. Do not understand me as proposing him as a man of genius, or a great general, but as far better in the present emergency than anyone we have available." Bragg also enclosed for Davis Hood's letter of the previous day, and dispatched the material to Richmond via private courier.

On July 16 Davis gave Johnston an opportunity to state his plan of action. The general's reply sealed his fate:

> As the enemy has double our number, we
> must be on the defensive. My plan of opera-
> tions must, therefore, depend upon that of the
> enemy. It is mainly to watch for an opportunity
> to fight to advantage. We are trying to put
> Atlanta in condition to be held for a day or two
> by the Georgia militia, that army movements
> may be freer and wider.

Johnston's response offered no indication that he would fight to hold Atlanta. To the contrary, it seemed to indicate that the city would be abandoned. Davis saw no alternative; Johnston had to be replaced.

With Bragg's strong, but qualified, endorsement of Hood, and the need for immediate aggressive action, Davis made perhaps his most controversial decision—he selected the young warrior to command the beleaguered army. Whatever Hood's role in the process, it likely had little bearing on Davis' decision.

On July 17 Adjutant and Inspector General Samuel Cooper telegraphed Johnston:

> Lieut. Gen. J.B. Hood has been commissioned to the temporary rank of general under the late law of Congress. I am directed by the Secretary of War to inform you that as you have failed to arrest the advance of the enemy to the vicinity of Atlanta, far in the interior of Georgia, and express no confidence that you can defeat or repel him, you are hereby relieved from the command of the Army and Department of Tennessee, which you will immediately turn over to General Hood.

The same day, Secretary of War James Seddon sent to Hood:

"You are charged with a great trust. You will, I know, test to the utmost your capacities to discharge it. Be no less wary than bold."

Before acknowledging the order, Hood joined Hardee and A.P. Stewart in asking Davis to retain Johnston through the present crisis. Davis replied, in effect, that such would defeat the purpose of the move: "A change of commanders, under existing circumstances, was regarded as so objectionable that I only accepted it as the alternative of continuing in a policy which had proved so disastrous. . . . The order has been executed, and I cannot suspend it without making the case worse than it was before the order was issued."

The announcement sent shock waves through the army. Reactions were largely negative, not that Hood lacked popularity but that Johnston held a special appeal. Brigadier General Clement Stevens wrote to the deposed general on the eighteenth:"The announcement that you are no longer to be our leader was received by officers and men in silence and deep sorrow. . . . We would hail with joy your return to command us." This sentiment spread throughout the Army of Tennessee. The rapport between Johnston and his army stood second only to that of Robert E. Lee and his men. Private Sam Watkins recalled: "It was like the end of the Southern Confederacy." This notwithstanding, Johnston had placed his beloved army in a very serious situation.

The Federals responded to the change with a mixture of apprehension and cautious optimism. Both McPherson and Schofield attended West Point with Hood. Schofield advised Sherman that Hood was "bold even to rashness, and courageous in the extreme." After discussing the change in Confederate leadership with his lieutenants, Sherman recalled: "We agreed that we ought to be unusually cautious and prepared at all times for sallies and for hard fighting, because Hood, though not deemed much of a scholar, or of great mental capacity, was undoubtedly a brave, determined, and rash man." Sherman believed that the change to Hood played into his hands. He welcomed the opportunity to meet the smaller enemy army in open battle, on terms of his choosing. But Grant more accurately estimated Confederate intentions in a telegram to Sherman: "Atlanta will be defended at all hazards and to the last extremity."

At thirty-three years of age, Hood became the eighth and youngest of the Confederate Army's generals of full rank. He had risen through the commissioned ranks, from first lieutenant to full general, in only three years, a feat achieved by no other man during the Civil War. On July 18 he issued a circular, announcing his acceptance of command:

> In obedience to orders from the War Department I assume command of this army and department. I feel the weight of the responsibility so suddenly and unexpectedly devolved upon me by this position, and shall bend all my energies and employ all my skill to meet its requirements. I look with confidence to your patriotism to stand by me, and rely upon your prowess to wrest your country from the grasp of the invader, entitling yourselves to the proud distinction of being called the deliverers of an oppressed people.

All speculation aside, whatever role the various machinations or maneuverings played in the ouster of Johnston and the promotion of Hood paled in comparison to the facts that confronted President Davis and the Confederacy. Johnston had not followed the directives of his government; he had failed to use his army's full force to oppose the Federal onslaught; and he appeared to be on the verge of the unthinkable—yielding Atlanta. Ultimately, Hood was selected for one reason—to fight—and no other available officer was better suited for the challenge.

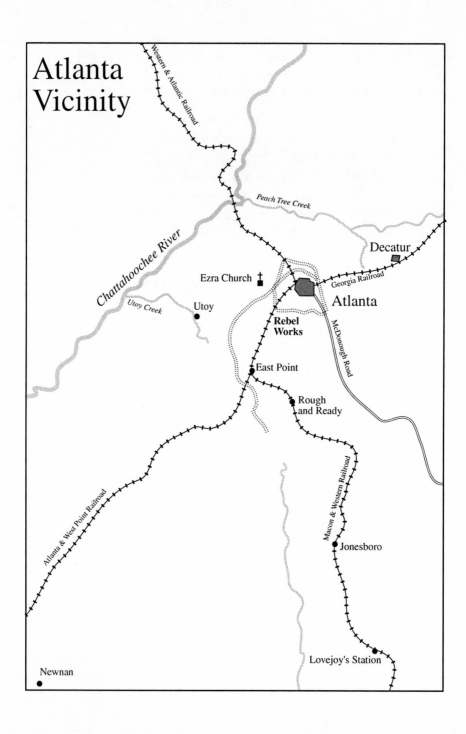

Atlanta Vicinity

4
THE LEE AND JACKSON SCHOOL

No general in the Civil War, with the possible exception of Robert E. Lee before Richmond in 1862, assumed command of a major army in a more desperate situation than did Hood. In each case, the officer in peril inherited his predicament from Johnston. With Federal armies moving on Atlanta from the north and east, Hood did not have the luxury of time. Whatever he did had to be done quickly. Unfortunately for Hood, his promotion came without instructions or even suggestions. He sought Johnston's counsel and believed he had the deposed general's assurance of advisory assistance, but, as Hood reported, Johnston "not only failed to comply with his promise, but, without a word of explanation or apology, left that evening for Macon, Georgia." Johnston had retreated yet again.

ALEXANDER P. STEWART

Born Tennessee 1821; Stewart was graduated from the U.S. Military Academy in 1842, twelfth in his class of fifty-six; commissioned 2d lieutenant and posted to artillery, he saw garrison duty and taught at the academy; he resigned his commission in 1845 to teach mathematics and phi-

losophy at Cumberland University and the University of Nashville; although an anti-secessionist, Stewart offered his services to the Confederacy, becoming a major of artillery; after seeing action in Kentucky and Missouri, he was appointed brigadier general in November 1861; he led a brigade at Shiloh, Perryville, Murfreesboro, and in the Tullahoma Campaign; elevated to major general in June 1863, Stewart commanded a division at Chickamauga, where he was slightly wounded, and at Chattanooga; during the Atlanta Campaign he assumed command of the Army of Mississippi (redesignated Stewart's Corps, Army of Tennessee) upon the death of General Leonidas Polk in June 1864; promoted to lieutenant general, Stewart led his corps with great distinction throughout the balance of the campaign, most notably at Peachtree Creek on July 20; he was also wounded in the ill-advised action at Ezra Church on July 28; Stewart became a true stalwart during General John B. Hood's disastrous Tennessee Campaign after which he joined General Joseph E. Johnston's command in North Carolina, where he surrendered what remained of the Army of Tennessee in April 1865; following the war, he returned to teaching and engaged in the insurance business; in 1874 he was named chancellor of the University of Mississippi, a position he held until 1886; he later became commissioner of the Chickamauga-Chattanooga National Military Park; he died at Biloxi, Mississippi, in 1908. General Stewart was among the Confederacy's most competent Western Theater commanders, participating in almost every battle fought by the Army of Tennessee.

Hood did, at least, know what was expected of him, namely, to fight. It was an expectation that he was more than willing to live up to. During almost three months of campaigning, the soldiers of the Army of Tennessee had become masters of the "Joe Johnston mode of warfare"—the strategic withdrawal. Hood had something altogether different in mind—a lesson in the "Lee and Jackson school." With his army quite literally backed against the wall, Hood had to act decisively. But the odds against him were even greater than Johnston had faced at Dalton—better than two to one.

Hood had at his disposal less than 50,000 effectives, including 10,000 cavalry and 1,500 Georgia militia. Of his infantry corps commanders, only Hardee was experienced in the position, but his resentment of Hood's appointment was no secret, even to the advancing Federals. One corps commander reported that "the assignment of Hood gives great dissatisfaction in Hardee's corps." A.P. Stewart had been promoted to lieutenant general to replace Polk, who had been killed in mid-June, and Major General Benjamin Franklin Cheatham assumed temporary command of Hood's former corps. Although veteran division commanders, neither was experienced in his new role. Thus Hood—with an army under untested leadership, and one that met his promotion with manifest displeasure, outnumbered and outgunned—faced the greatest threat yet to the Confederacy's continued existence.

While Grant paid a heavy price in blood for every inch he gained in Virginia, Sherman had moved more than one hundred miles into Georgia with comparatively little loss of life. He counted 17,000 total casualties in two months of continuous campaigning—fewer than Grant had suffered in two days of fighting in the Wilderness. Sherman's campaign, though often frustrating, had brought him to the very gates of Atlanta with a force that still numbered more than 105,000 men. Thomas's Army of the Cumberland, itself 10,000 men larger than Hood's entire army, moving on Atlanta from the north, approached Peachtree Creek, the last natural impediment of consequence between the Cumberlanders and their trophy. McPherson's Army of the Tennessee and Schofield's Army of the Ohio, swinging wide to Thomas's left, bore down on Decatur from the northeast. Although Hood's reputation prompted caution, Sherman's armies continued to press closer.

One of the war's great prizes now stood within Sherman's reach. Atlanta was still a young city in 1864. Incorporated in 1843, the "Gate City's" population had more than doubled during the war to 22,000, making it the second largest city still held by the Confederates (only Richmond was larger). Four railroads met at Atlanta. The Western & Atlantic running north to Chattanooga and the Georgia Railroad running eastward through Decatur and on to Augusta were now cut by the Federal advance. The Macon & Western that entered the city from the south, and the Atlanta & West Point that extended

BENJAMIN FRANKLIN CHEATHAM

Born Tennessee 1820; Frank Cheatham served credibly during the Mexican War, most notably as colonel of Tennessee volunteers; after the war he journeyed to California to participate in the Gold Rush of 1849; returning to Tennessee in 1853, he engaged in planting and became a major general in the state militia; following Tennessee's secession, he entered Confederate service as a brigadier general in July 1861; he played a major role in the Confederate victory at Belmont, Missouri, in November; promoted to major general in March 1862, Cheatham led a division with great distinction at Shiloh and in General Braxton Bragg's Kentucky Campaign; after an ineffectual performance at Murfreesboro, he joined the group of Army of Tennessee generals who actively opposed Bragg's continued command of the army, a position that intensified after the Tullahoma Campaign; Cheatham and his division fought westward into Alabama, brought supplies for Hood's army and maintained communications to the rest of the Confederacy.

Atlanta also had become a major manufacturing center and military depot. Its ironworks produced cannon, armor plating, and rail; an armory produced vital ammunition and other equipment; and a pistol factory turned out small arms. The Army of Tennessee's Quartermaster and Commissary Departments occupied dozens of buildings and warehouses. Atlanta also housed several major hospital facilities, banks, and food production operations. But, as the war dragged on, crime became a serious problem, exacerbated by runaway slaves, deserters, and transient riffraff. Overcrowding brought dangerous sanitary conditions. Atlanta felt the burden of war long before Federal guns came to bear on the city. Its loss would be a crippling blow to the Confederacy.

well at Chickamauga and helped cover the Confederate retreat following the collapse at Missionary Ridge; during the Atlanta Campaign of 1864, although still a division commander, he was repeatedly called upon to command a corps and did so with mixed effect during the pivotal Battle of Atlanta; he headed General W.J. Hardee's former corps during General J.B. Hood's Tennessee Campaign; he was blamed by Hood for allowing the Federals to escape a trap at Spring Hill, Tennessee, and paid the price when his corps suffered horribly in the bloody Battle of Franklin in November 1864 and at Nashville the following month; in 1865 he led what remained of his corps to North Carolina, where it served under General J.E. Johnston until surrendering in April; after the war he returned to his Tennessee farm and served as superintendent of the Tennessee State Prison; in 1885 he became postmaster of Nashville; he died there in September 1886; given to heavy drinking and profanity, he was nonetheless extremely popular with his men and commanded considerable political influence; although he led a corps for a lengthy period, he was never given the appropriate rank of lieutenant general; still, he was an able, often outstanding commander, whose division ranked among the best in Confederate service.

Hood wasted little time in exercising his mandate to defend the city. Aware that Thomas was moving on Peachtree Creek and separated from the rest of Sherman's force, Hood planned to strike the isolated Army of the Cumberland just after it crossed the creek and before it could entrench. Hood's force held a line about a mile south of Peachtree Creek and three miles north of Atlanta. The five-mile front extended in a rough arc from the Western & Atlantic railroad on the left to just north of the Georgia Railroad on the right. Hood's plan called for an *en echelon* attack by division. Hardee's Corps, holding the center of the Rebel line, would advance right to left, followed by Stewart's. Cheatham would extend his line to the

OLIVER O. HOWARD

Born Maine 1830; graduated from Bowdoin College in 1850, he entered the U.S. Military Academy and was graduated in 1854, fourth in his class of forty-six that included J.E.B. Stuart and S.D. Lee; commissioned a 2d lieutenant of ordnance, he spent much of his pre-war career teaching mathematics at West Point; following the outbreak of the Civil War, Howard resigned from the regular army as 1st lieutenant to become colonel of the 3d Maine Infantry; he commanded a brigade during the First Battle of Bull Run and was promoted to brigadier general of volunteers in September 1861; he lost his right arm to a wound received at Seven Pines during the Peninsular Campaign in March 1862, but was back in action by the end of July; he commanded a division at Antietam and Fredericksburg; he was, in the meantime, promoted to major general of volunteers in November 1862; the following spring he commanded the Eleventh Corps at Chancellorsville and was routed by Confederate General T.J. "Stonewall" Jackson's brilliant attack; Howard's right to cover the eastward approaches to Atlanta and Hardee's flank, while Major General G.W. Smith's Georgia militia manned the city's eastside defenses, and Wheeler's cavalry operated against McPherson and Schofield in the vicinity of Decatur.

Before midnight on July 19 Hood assembled his corps commanders and explained his plan. The attack was to begin at 1 P.M. the next day. Following the example of Robert E. Lee, Hood outlined the objective and issued the orders but entrusted his corps commanders with their execution. Hardee's Corps would surprise Thomas, hitting the Federal flank and rear, then Stewart would attack and drive the enemy into the creek.

corps was again handled roughly at Gettysburg but he received credit—and the Thanks of Congress—for selecting the ground upon which the Federal army made its stand; transferred to the Western Theater, he served at Chattanooga in November 1863; the following spring he directed the Fourth Corps during the early stages of the Atlanta Campaign; after the death of General J.B. McPherson in July 1864, Howard was selected by General W.T. Sherman to head the Army of the Tennessee, which he led for the balance of the campaign, on Sherman's March to the Sea, and in the Carolinas Campaign; promoted to brigadier general in the regular army and breveted major general, he also was received the Medal of Honor (in 1893) for Seven Pines; a devoted abolitionist and deeply religious, Howard in May 1865 became commissioner of the Freedman's Bureau and in 1874 helped establish Howard University; returning to active duty, he directed peace efforts with the Apaches and led the arduous pursuit of Chief Joseph's Nez Perce before becoming superintendent of West Point; promoted to major general in 1886, he commanded the Department of the East until his retirement in 1894; thereafter he wrote and lectured extensively and attended to the numerous humanitarian causes with which he was involved; General Howard died at Burlington, Vermont, in 1909; a dedicated and courageous soldier, he overcame early disasters to become a solid, though never outstanding, commander.

It was a solid plan derived from the "Lee and Jackson School," and not a recklessly conceived frontal assault as would later be claimed. As Brigadier General Winfield Scott Featherston of

JOSEPH HOOKER

Born Massachusetts 1814; graduated U.S. Military Academy 1837, twenty-ninth in his class of fifty cadets; brevetted 2d lieutenant assigned to artillery; on frontier duty, fought in Seminole wars, and held a staff assignment at West Point; served conspicuously in Mexican War, earning three brevets; captain 1848; resigned his commission 1853; engaged in farming

in California and served as colonel in the state militia; offered his services to the Union at the outbreak of the Civil War but was initially snubbed owing to poor relations with General Winfield Scott; commissioned brigadier general U.S. Volunteers May 1861; led a division in the Peninsular Campaign and at Second Bull Run; major general U.S. Volunteers May 1862; commanded First Corps and was wounded at Antietam September 1862; promoted brigadier general U.S. Army to date from the battle; named to command the Army of the Potomac January 1863; routed by badly outnumbered Confederates at Chancellorsville, but received the thanks of Congress for his subsequent defense of Washington May 1863; relieved at his own request in June; sent West, took command of the newly formed Twentieth Corps Army of the Cumberland, which he led with great success at Chattanooga and during the Atlanta Campaign; resigned when overlooked for the command of the Army of the Tennessee following the death of General James B. McPherson; for the balance of the war he exercised various departmental commands; brevetted major general U.S. Army for Chattanooga victory; remained in the regular army until his retirement in 1868; died 1879. Although the disaster at Chancellorsville tainted his career, General Hooker proved to be a competent combat officer at division and corps level. While he hated his sobriquet "Fighting Joe," it was nonetheless appropriate.

Stewart's Corps remarked in his official report, "I thought the battle had been well planned, and heard it spoken of by my associates in arms in terms of commendation."

Hood had Thomas where he wanted him and confidently anticipated victory. The Federal deployment "afforded," as Hood recalled, "one of the most favorable occasions for complete victory which could have been offered."

Thomas, finding little opposition, began crossing his army on the nineteenth. Believing that an attack, if planned, would fall on the smaller force of McPherson and Schofield, Sherman ordered Thomas to send Major General O.O. Howard's Fourth Corps to bolster Schofield's single corps. On the morning of the twentieth Major General John Palmer's Fourteenth Corps, the first to complete the crossing, cautiously formed on the right and dug in. Brigadier General John Newton's Division, retained from Howard's Corps, crossed and formed on the left. Major General Joseph "Fighting Joe" Hooker's Corps crossed last and deployed between Palmer and Newton. Brigadier General John Geary's Division, along with Newton's, moved to an advanced position along a small ridge, awaiting the arrival of the divisions of Brigadier Generals Alpheus Williams and William Ward before continuing the advance.

As Hooker's men crossed Peachtree Creek, Hood received word from Wheeler that McPherson and Schofield were much closer than expected. Consequently, Hood ordered Cheatham to shift eastward so as to cover the Decatur Road. The shift necessitated a similar move from Hardee and Stewart so that Hardee's flank remained covered. The redeployment proved a bungling affair as Cheatham moved farther than ordered, forcing Hardee and Stewart to do the same. At 1 P.M., the projected time of attack, the moves were still in progress, but Hardee failed to report the delay to Hood.

The shift actually improved Hardee's position, extending it well past Newton's uncovered flank. The delay was of small consequence, as Thomas's cautious advance had gained little

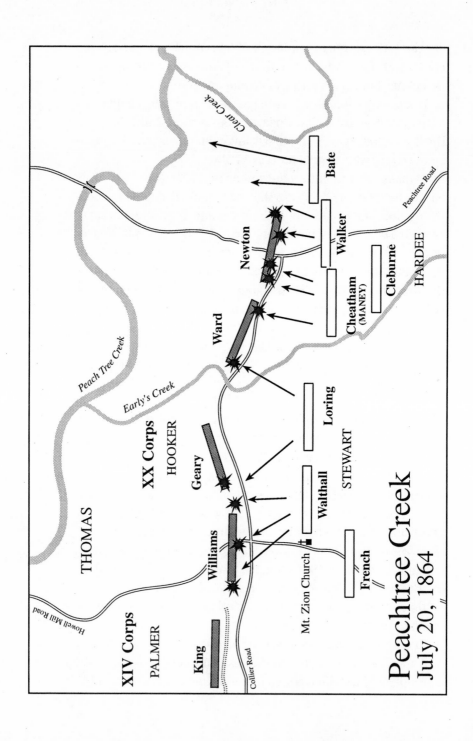

Peachtree Creek
July 20, 1864

ground. Owing to the dense woods and hilly terrain, neither army could see the other, but the Confederates knew Thomas's position, while Thomas had only Sherman's assurance that the attack, if it came, would take place to the east. The element of surprise remained very much intact.

Finally, after 3 P.M., Hardee prepared to attack, with Major General William Bate's Division on the right, followed by Major General W.H.T. Walker's, and Cheatham's, commanded by Brigadier General George Maney. Strangely, in what was likely to be the army's most important battle of the war, Hardee held arguably the best division in the army, Cleburne's, in reserve. Bate's Division began the *en echelon* advance but soon became disorganized and lost its bearing in the dense underbrush, never making meaningful contact. Walker's Division, spearheaded by Clement Stevens's Georgia Brigade, struck the enemy line in a spirited effort, before well directed artillery halted the assault. General Stevens fell mortally wounded while directing a second charge. Maney's Division advanced in a disjointed and ineffective effort that was beaten back by the partially entrenched Yankees.

Stewart's Corps then took up the fight. Advancing more in the spirit that Hood had prescribed for a "bold and persistent attack," Stewart's men appeared prepared to "carry everything, at all hazards." Major General W.W. Loring's Division hit with the greatest effect. General Featherston's Mississippi Brigade struck Ward's advancing division unprepared, while Brigadier General Thomas Scott's Brigade fell upon Geary's front and flank. The furious Rebel attack threatened to breach the Federal center.

The stunned Yankees rallied handsomely. With no pressure coming from Hardee's front, Ward could throw his entire division at Featherston's single brigade. Colonel David Ireland's Brigade from Geary's Division launched a savage counterattack against Scott's breakthrough. Both Rebel brigades fought on, yielding ground grudgingly.

As Geary's and Ward's men worked to restore their front, Confederate Major General Edward Walthall's Division hit Williams's still deploying Federals. Colonel Edward O'Neal's Brigade and the Arkansas Brigade of Brigadier General Daniel Reynolds, advancing undetected through the covering woods, surprised their enemy with murderous effect. But, here again, Federal artillery stymied the Rebel advance. Among the Confederate dead was Walthall's chief of artillery, Major William Preston—the brother of Hood's fiancee.

Although Stewart's attack was well delivered and inflicted considerable damage on the Twentieth Corps, it lacked the weight to exploit its gains. Each of Stewart's divisions had only two brigades in the line of battle and no reserves, each having sent a brigade to man Atlanta's westside defenses. Stewart, wanting to press the attack, sent to Hardee for help; Hardee offered Cleburne's Division. Stewart also recalled a brigade from the westside defenses to join in a renewed assault—one he hoped would give the Confederacy the victory it desperately needed.

Stewart never got to launch the attack. The mounting crisis arising from McPherson's fast approaching columns forced Hood to summon Cleburne's Division to strengthen the eastside defense. By 6 P.M. the battle had played out, although sporadic fighting along the Peachtree front lasted well into the evening.

Hood's bold attack had failed, and he believed he knew the reason—Hardee. Hood, who measured the commitment of his men in terms of casualties, found in Hardee's losses evidence that his corps did not engage the enemy with vigor equal to the demands of the moment. In his report Hood charged: "Hardee failed to push the attack as ordered." Whether intentionally or not, Hardee had not distinguished himself. Only Walker's Division made a substantial impact on the surprised enemy, while Stewart, with far fewer troops and less surprise, inflicted serious damage. Stewart's losses in his four attacking brigades numbered 1,400, compared to about 1,000 in Hardee's ten. "I cannot but think," Stewart maintained in his report, "had the plan of the battle, as I understood it, been carried out fully, we would have achieved a great success."

Union losses seemed to confirm Hood's thesis. The three divisions that contested Stewart's attack counted close to 1,700 casualties, while Newton's Division, upon which most of Hardee's advance fell, reported only 102. Whatever the case, Hood's attack ended in defeat. The sole consolation was that Thomas's advance had been, at least temporarily, stymied.

Sherman was unaware of the danger Thomas faced on Peachtree Creek. Content in his belief that any attack would be directed at McPherson's army, Sherman passed the day maligning the Cumberlanders' slow advance. Not until the battle was decided did Sherman learn of Thomas's fight. Only then did he realize that the bulk of Hood's army opposed Thomas, and that as at Resaca, McPherson had been deterred by a much smaller force. Atlanta had been Sherman's for the taking; McPherson had missed the chance. For the Army of the Cumberland, on the other hand, caution had paid off. Their reputation for slowness notwithstanding, Thomas's men were among the best fighters in either army. As he had done almost a year before at Chickamauga, Thomas displayed quiet competence. Sherman might complain about "Old Slow Trot," but Thomas had justified his other sobriquet: the "Rock of Chickamauga."

As for Hood, his first effort at emulating his mentor Lee ended in disappointment. Hood's physical limitations may have been a factor. Although, his condition had improved enough to allow him to ride a horse rather well, his mobility remained restricted. He could not exercise the close supervision of the battle that his complicated plan demanded. Also, he had left the execution of his orders to his subordinates, as Lee often had, and did not manage his army closely. This proved costly. But his plan had been a good one, and had almost brought the desired result. Later charges that he had foolishly flung his army into a costly frontal assault were groundless. His 13 percent casualty rate at Peachtree Creek was comparatively low by Civil War standards. General Featherston commented that had the plan been delivered as ordered, "I then believe, and still believe, the victory would have been a brilliant one."

But other than slowing Thomas, the battle had done nothing to relieve the pressure on Atlanta, and Hood now had to face the threat posed by McPherson. The stage was set for another, yet bolder exercise in the "Lee and Jackson School" of warfare.

5
BRILLIANT BUT DISASTROUS

Hood had little time to dwell on the disappointment at Peachtree Creek. "The failure of the 20th," he wrote, "rendered urgent the most active measures, in order to save Atlanta." With McPherson's army less than two miles from central Atlanta, the new commander turned his attention to the east. Fortunately for Hood, McPherson failed to press the issue. He still believed that he faced the bulk of the Rebel army, although in fact, until Cleburne's Division arrived from the Peachtree front, McPherson's army of 25,000 faced only 3,500 harried cavalrymen from Wheeler's command. The approaching Yankees contented themselves with lobbing shells into the city.

Hood had dodged a bullet when McPherson failed to seize the opportunity presented him, but he could not count on such good fortune to continue. Accordingly, he devised a most ambitious plan—starkly reminiscent of Jackson's brilliant maneuver at Chancellorsville. He planned to pull Stewart's and Cheatham's Corps, along with Smith's militia, back to a new defensive line outside Atlanta to block the approach of Thomas and Schofield. Hardee's Corps would then pull out of line, march south through the city and swing eastward to fall on McPherson's exposed flank, south of the Decatur Road. Wheeler, with a large force of cavalry, was to strike McPherson's supply train at Decatur. Once Hardee rolled up the Union flank, Cheatham would advance to complete the destruction.

Sherman spent the twenty-first consolidating his forces. Thomas held the Peachtree front on the north while Schofield moved into the gap between Thomas and McPherson on the east. McPherson's pressure on the east resulted in the capture of Bald Hill, a slight, yet important elevation—but again, he could have had more. For most of the day he faced only cavalry and Cleburne's Division, before another Confederate division, Maney's, arrived late in the afternoon. The Rebels not only held their ground, but, more important, kept McPherson where Hood wanted him.

Informed during the night of Hood's withdrawal from his outer works and of Rebel troops moving south through the city, Sherman believed Hood to be evacuating Atlanta, as he had expected. The Federal commander then issued orders for a general pursuit by Thomas and McPherson, while Schofield occupied the city. As the sun rose on the twenty-second Sherman found that the Confederate Army had gone nowhere, but still, he did not expect a fight. He simply canceled the planned pursuit and issued orders for the envelopment of Atlanta to continue.

On the Confederate side, Hood's choice of Hardee's Corps as the flanking column presented several problems. "I selected Hardee for this duty," Hood wrote years afterward, "because Cheatham had, at the time, but little experience as a corps commander, and Stewart had been heavily engaged the day previous [July 20]." But Hardee too had been engaged at Peachtree Creek, albeit not to the commander's satisfaction. Also two of his divisions, Cleburne's and Maney's had been heavily engaged opposite McPherson on the twenty-first, and could not disengage until nightfall. Not until well after midnight were all of Hardee's men in motion. Even though Hood and Hardee agreed to shorten the march, it would still take all night, and then the men would be forced to fight, perhaps all day, without rest. It was also July in Georgia, oppressively hot and, after an evening shower, brutally humid.

Within Atlanta, during the long night of the twenty-first, the steady southward procession of troops through the city triggered a wave of panic. Assuming the movement of so many soldiers indicated an evacuation, hundreds of citizens fled the city rather than face Sherman's wrath. But others, including soldiers, joined in a horrifying display of vandalism and violence—pillaging stores, saloons, and residences. "Cavalry robbers broke into the store," one disgusted observer noted, "and stole everything that they took a fancy to."

Following its grueling all-night march, Hardee's Corps was not in position to attack at daybreak as planned. Impeded by a variety of natural obstructions, Hardee could not launch his assault until after noon. The delay, though hardly avoidable, proved costly.

Although he did not expect an attack, the ever-cautious McPherson had recalled Major General Grenville Dodge's Sixteenth Corps from Decatur. As a result, the divisions of Brigadier generals John Fuller and Thomas Sweeny had formed behind McPherson's exposed left flank just prior to Hardee's attack.

About 1 P.M. on July 22 the Battle of Atlanta began in earnest as Hardee's divisions moved forward. Despite the unexpected presence of the Sixteenth Corps, the attack achieved surprise, but the effect was short-lived. Before his division even engaged its enemy, General W.H.T. Walker was

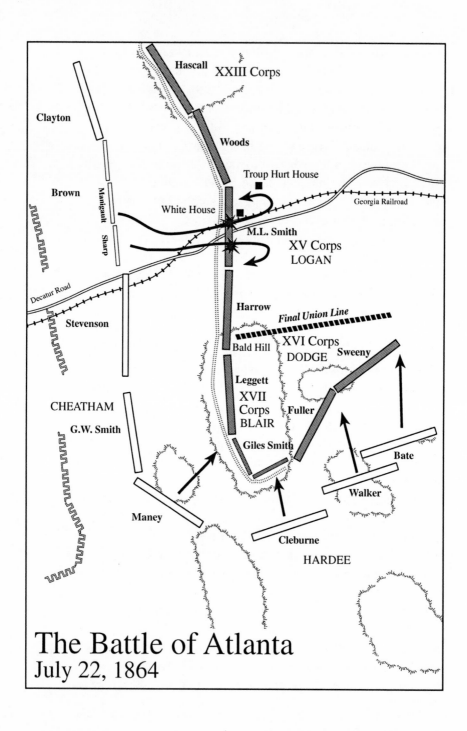

The Battle of Atlanta
July 22, 1864

killed by an alert Federal picket as he examined his front. Bate's Division led the advance, followed by Walker's, now commanded by aged and infirm Brigadier General Hugh Mercer, but after a difficult approach, the exhausted Rebels were repulsed by the hastily deployed divisions of Sweeny and Fuller, backed by canister fire from well-placed Federal batteries.

With Dodge's front apparently secured, McPherson, who had arrived shortly after the shooting began, quickly moved to examine the gap between Dodge and Major General Frank Blair's Seventeenth Corps. After sending for a brigade to fill the gap, he galloped on to find Blair. He instead rode into skirmishers from Cleburne's oncoming Confederate division and was killed as he tried to escape. Word of McPherson's death shocked Sherman, but he wasted no time in passing the command of the Army of the Tennessee to Major General John A. Logan. Much to Sherman's relief, McPherson's pocketbook containing a letter from the commanding general outlining future plans was recovered from a Confederate prisoner. Across the battle lines, the news of McPherson's death brought no pleasure."No soldier fell in the enemy's ranks," Hood wrote of his one-time classmate and friend, "whose loss caused me equal regret."

Cleburne's Division, soon joined by Maney's, moved to exploit the gap that McPherson had sought to close. Determined Rebel assaults penetrated the gap, falling on the Federal flank and gaining considerable headway against the partially entrenched Seventeenth Corps. Brigadier General Giles Smith's Division, under severe pressure, put up an equally determined resistance. With the assistance of Brigadier General Mortimer Leggett's Division and the timely arrival of Brigadier General Charles Walcutt's Brigade from the Fifteenth Corps, Smith's men held. Logan, arriving on the scene, worked to stabilize the line and to close the interval between Dodge and Blair. But before this could be accomplished, the Rebels resumed their attack. Again they struck Blair's front and flank,

FRANCIS P. BLAIR, JR.

Born Kentucky 1821; graduated from Princeton in 1841, Frank Blair studied law at Transylvania University in Kentucky and opened a practice in St.Louis; he staunchly opposed secession and the expansion of slavery into the territories and actively worked against both; he served two terms in the U.S. House of Representatives and was a strong supporter of Abraham Lincoln; his brother Montgomery was Lincoln's first postmaster general; he led Missouri's pro-Union faction and with Nathaniel Lyon directed the seizure of the St.Louis arsenal and pro-secession forces at Camp Jackson; largely at his own expense he raised seven regiments for Federal service and in August 1862 was appointed brigadier general of U.S. Volunteers; promoted to major general in November, he commanded a brigade and then a division during the Vicksburg Campaign; during the Chattanooga Campaign he headed the Fifteenth Corps, Army of the Tennessee; as commander of the Seventeenth Corps, he performed with marked distinction during the Atlanta Campaign of 1864, and played a major role in the July Battle of Atlanta; he continued to direct the Seventeenth Corps during General W.T. Sherman's March to the Sea and in the Carolinas Campaign of 1865; he resigned his volunteer commission in November 1865; at war's end Blair was financially ruined, having spent his personal fortune in support of the Union; he also fell into disfavor with radical Republicans for his opposition to heavy-handed reconstruction policies; Blair, who favored more lenient readmission terms for Confederate states, was twice nominated for governmental posts by President Andrew Johnson but failed to win confirmation from the vindictive Senate; finally in 1871 he was selected to fill an unexpired term in the U.S. Senate but long plagued by poor heath he resigned in 1873 and died at St. Louis in 1875; he was one of several civilian or "political" generals to render excellent service during the Civil War.

but the uncoordinated nature of the assault allowed the Federals to face one crisis at a time. Finally, concentrated artillery fire wore down the attackers. By 3 P.M. Hardee's attack seemed to have played out.

Disappointed by Hardee's lack of success, Hood ordered Cheatham, commanding Hood's old corps, to demonstrate against the Fifteenth Corps front to keep the enemy from massing on Hardee. But by 4 P.M., Hardee again was advancing, determined to capture the Bald Hill manned by Giles Smith's and Leggett's Divisions. Brigadier General Daniel Govan's Arkansas Brigade and the Tennesseans of Brigadier General Alfred Vaughn's Brigade spearheaded the renewed effort. After driving Smith's line backward until it formed an angle at Bald Hill, the relentless Confederates focused on the all-important hill. Intense fighting lasted past sundown but ended with the Federals still occupying the hill. Only by herculean efforts did the Yankees hold—it was far too close for comfort.

Tennessean Sam Watkins of Maney's command recalled the carnage he encountered in the assaults on the Bald Hill:

> On the final charge that was made, I was shot in the ankle and heel of my foot. I crawled into their abandoned ditch, which then seemed full and running over with our wounded soldiers. I dodged behind the embankment to get out of the raking fire that was ripping through the bushes, and tearing up the ground. Here I felt safe. The firing raged in front; we could hear the shout of the charge and the clash of battle. While I was sitting here, a cannon ball came tearing down the works, cutting a soldier's head off, spattering his brains all over my face and bosom, and mangling and tearing four or five others to shreds. As a wounded

horse was being led off, a cannon ball struck
him, and he was literally ripped open, falling in
the very place I had just moved from.

Buoyed by Hardee's resumption of the attack on the right,
Hood ordered Cheatham to escalate his demonstration into a
full-scale assault. Two of Cheatham's divisions were under new
and untested commanders. Major General Henry Clayton commanded Stewart's former Division, and Brigadier General John
C. Brown had temporarily taken over for Hindman, who had
left the army after sustaining an eye injury. Cheatham's deployment had Clayton's Division on the left, Brown's in the center,
and Major General Carter Stevenson's on the right.

G.W. Smith's Georgia militia formed a link between
Cheatham and Hardee. Stevenson's punchless division
advanced and soon withdrew. Smith's militia, keying on
Stevenson, had no choice but to follow the example.

Brown's Division took up the assault, advancing eastward
up the Georgia Railroad. Exploiting a serious Federal oversight, the brigades of Brigadier General Arthur Manigault and
Colonel Jacob Sharp charged through a virtually unprotected
railroad cut and wagon road that bisected the Fifteenth Corps'
2d Division, temporarily commanded by Brigadier General
Joseph Lightburn. Manigault's and Sharp's men split the center
of Lightburn's line, capturing two sections of artillery and
gaining possession of a commanding two-story white house
just behind the Federal line. Manigault pushed on, routing
Colonel Wells Jones's Brigade and capturing the two-story
brick Troup House and Captain Francis Degress's four-gun
Illinois Battery, the same guns that had lobbed the first shells
into Atlanta.

Sharp's Mississippians then hit Colonel James Martin's
Brigade's flank, routing the brigade and gaining another sec-
tion of artillery. Brown's remaining brigades joined the effort,
with less effect, south of the railroad. But Brown's attack had

ripped a huge hole in the Federal line, and threatened to do much worse. Inexplicably, at the height of the advance, Brown ordered Manigault and Sharp to withdraw, then countermanded the order. Confused by the conflicting orders, Manigault

ARTHUR M. MANIGAULT

Born South Carolina 1824 to a prominent family; a commission merchant and planter in and near Charleston, he was active in the state militia and served in the Mexican War; following the secession of South Carolina, he entered Confederate service; as a staff officer under General P.G.T. Beauregard he was present at the bombardment of Fort Sumter; selected colonel of the 10th South Carolina Infantry; sent to the Western Theater, Manigault's regiment joined the Army of Tennessee in May 1862; after directing a brigade at Murfreesboro, he was promoted to brigadier general in April 1863; commanded a brigade in General James Longstreet's Wing at Chickamauga in September 1863; led his brigade at Chattanooga and throughout the Atlanta Campaign; during the Battle of Atlanta in July 1864 Manigault's Brigade spearheaded an assault that pierced the Federal line and threatened to divide the Union Army; during General J.B. Hood's ill-fated Tennessee Campaign, Manigault received a severe head wound at the Battle of Franklin in November 1864, ending his service to the Confederacy; after the war he returned to planti-

ng; in 1880 he became the adjutant and inspector general of South Carolina; General Manigault died in 1886 of the lasting effects of his Franklin wound. He was a capable commander and his brigade was among the finest in the Army of Tennessee. His memoir, *A Carolinian Goes to War*, not published until 1983, is an excellent account of activities in the Western Theater. The breakthrough of Manigault's Brigade during the Battle of Atlanta is the focus of that city's Cyclorama exhibit.

pleaded for reinforcements. Although Federal pressure was building, Manigault and Sharp held. Finally, two of Clayton's brigades arrived to bolster the stalled advance. It was too little too late. The golden opportunity had passed. The inexperience in the high command of Cheatham's Corps had indeed come into play.

Sherman watched the Rebel attack on his front with growing anxiety. After ordering Schofield to send his artillery, Sherman personally directed its placement. Major General Morgan Smith, now commanding Logan's Fifteenth Corps and desperately trying to restore his line, ordered a counterattack to retake the Troup House. In response to the crisis befalling his own corps, "Black Jack" Logan, who had been following

JOHN A. LOGAN

Born Illinois 1826; Logan studied law and served as a volunteer officer during the Mexican War; he entered the Illinois legislature and in 1858 was elected to the U.S. House of Representatives; a Democrat, he whole-heartedly supported the Union; during the First Battle of Bull Run, while still a civilian, he picked up a musket and joined the fighting; he then raised a regiment that became the 31st Illinois and he became its colonel; he fought at Belmont and was wounded at Fort Donelson; promoted to brigadier general, U.S. Volunteers, in March 1862, he resigned his congressional seat and returned to action during the operations at Corinth, Mississippi; promoted to major general of volunteers in November 1862, he commanded a division in the Army of the Tennessee during the Vicksburg Campaign; he commanded the Fifteenth Corps, Army of the Tennessee, during the Atlanta Campaign of 1864; when General J.B. McPherson was killed during the Battle of Atlanta, Logan assumed command of the army, rallying the shattered force to victory;

the events on the far left, rode the length of the Federal line, trailing a brigade from the Sixteenth Corps. As the fire from massed Federal artillery pounded the Rebel position, Logan personally rallied his shattered command and directed an all-out effort to restore the line. "Logan, with fire in his eyes," recalled an Ohio soldier, "came dashing down the line at the head of a fresh brigade. I and others joined them, and with bayonets fixed we charged upon the enemy." The Federal counterattack struck as Manigault and Sharp, reluctantly obeying Brown's second order to withdraw, abandoned their hard-won positions. The Yankees easily drove Clayton's brigades, regaining the Troup House and most of their captured guns, including Degress's prized 20-pounder Parrot rifles. "Captain DeGress,"

despite his performance and his acknowledged ability on the battlefield, General W.T. Sherman passed over Logan, who was not a West Pointer, for permanent command of the Army of the Tennessee, opting instead for General O.O. Howard; although embittered, Logan returned to his corps and led it with great skill for the remainder of the campaign; after the fall of Atlanta, he took a leave to campaign for President Abraham Lincoln's reelection; he rejoined his command at Savannah and led the Fifteenth Corps throughout the Carolinas Campaign of 1865; after leading the Army of the Tennessee in the Grand Review at Washington, he resigned his volunteer commission in August 1865; declining a brigadier generalcy in the regular army, he returned to politics as a Republican; he served in both the House and Senate and was an unsuccessful vice presidential candidate in 1884; dedicated to veteran's affairs, he was prominent in the Grand Army of the Republic; he also wrote extensively on the war, including *The Volunteer Soldier of America* that extolled the virtues of the volunteer over the professional soldier; General Logan died at Washington in 1886. Clearly one of the most effective of the so-called "political generals," Logan was an outstanding combat commander; his lack of a West Point pedigree no doubt cost him an army command.

remarked an observer, "soon came up and threw his arms around his pet guns and cried for joy." Sherman had escaped a catastrophe.

Although fighting continued until nightfall, the battle that had come so close to being a spectacular Confederate victory ended in bloody defeat. As at Peachtree Creek, a promising attack had not been exploited. General Manigault voiced pride and disappointment—both justifiable—in the achievement of his brigade:

> Take it all in all, this was one of the most spirited and dashing contests that the brigade ever fought, and they won much praise for their obstinacy and valor. I do not remember any instance during the war when so small a force captured so many pieces of artillery in one fight (16), the same being protected by works. . . . Much disgust was expressed at the time and afterwards, when all the events of the day were known, and it was believed that had a competent commander been present, the result of the day's work would have been far different. Instead of ten or twelve pieces of artillery, a few colors ...it might have culminated in a brilliant victory.

No doubt, the inexperience of Brown and Clayton was a contributing factor, but even had the confusion been avoided, Cheatham's Corps lacked the weight to capitalize on its gains. Hardee's Corps, at least Cleburne's and Maney's Divisions, made up for its poor showing of two days before, but fatigue, heat, and again, the lack of available support proved costly. Wheeler struck Decatur as planned, but largely failed to disrupt the Federal rear. Confederate casualties approached 6,000, close to 20 percent of the men engaged. Still, Hood's army had inflicted substantial damage. While not victorious, it had stopped Sherman's advance. Atlanta remained in Confederate hands.

Sherman, having anxiously observed the desperate battle, could only welcome its conclusion with relief. He had not expected the Rebel onslaught, and if it had not been for the inspired leadership of many of his generals and the tenacity of his soldiers, the battle could have had a much different outcome. The Army of the Tennessee had suffered 4,000 casualties, including its commander. In McPherson, Sherman had lost not only his most trusted lieutenant but also a close personal friend: no victory that included such a loss could be considered complete. Moreover, as had occurred two days previously, Sherman had fought a defensive battle with just one portion of his army. Content to allow the Army of the Tennessee to fight it out on its own, he had kept Thomas's huge army relatively dormant when it outnumbered the troops in its front by at least five to one. "As it was," Frank Blair wrote years afterward, "we congratulated ourselves on being able to hold our ground, and we felt satisfied that Hood's Army could not stand much longer the terrible losses it was suffering from brilliant but disastrous movements." But Hood still held Atlanta and now showed no intention of surrendering it.

At 10:30 P.M. Hood dispatched an ambiguous telegram to Richmond that hinted at victory. In closing he stated, "Our troops fought with great gallantry." But the general had not had a good day. He watched "with astonishment and bitter disappointment" as his bold plan unraveled. Again Hardee bore the brunt of Hood's indictment. "Hardee failed to entirely turn the enemy's left as directed," he reported. Years later, in his memoirs, Hood continued his attack, maintaining that Hardee lacked the "boldness requisite for offensive warfare." At least as far as the action on July 22 was concerned, this was an unfair judgement.

Hardee was not Stonewall Jackson, nor was Hood Lee. And despite all his efforts to make it so, Hood could not duplicate the magic of Second Manassas or Chancellorsville. This, he maintained, was due to his army's long exposure to Johnston's handling. "Had these same forces, at my disposal in these battles [Peachtree Creek and Atlanta], been previously handled according to the Lee and Jackson school," Hood maintained, "they would have routed the Federal Army." Thus Hood made excuses that need not have been made. His plan was sound; its execution, if not flawless, showed great determination. The error came in setting goals that his army could not attain. But, then again, the situation demanded boldness and, despite the odds, the plan almost worked. Sherman would be much more careful in days to come. The largest and bloodiest battle of the campaign had been fought.

6

No Decided Advantage

Following the carnage of the twenty-second, Hood pulled his force into Atlanta's defenses to await Sherman's next move. He believed the events of the past few days had greatly improved the army's morale and "had the subsequent effect of arresting desertions almost entirely." Perhaps, after the long withdrawal and the repeated inability to thwart Sherman's advance, the Battle of Atlanta was a victory of sorts. But after fighting two major battles in forty-eight hours the Army of Tennessee badly needed rest, and with Federal gunners lobbing shells into the city, rest would not come easily.

The events of the past week necessitated several changes in the army. Brigadier General W.W. Mackall, the army's chief of staff and a loyal Johnston man, was relieved and replaced by artillery chief Brigadier General Francis Shoup. Lieutenant General Stephen D. Lee arrived from Mississippi to assume command of Hood's old corps. Cheatham, that corps' temporary commander, returned to his division in Hardee's Corps. The division of the fallen Walker was broken up and distributed between Hardee's remaining divisions. Major General Patton Anderson was summoned from Florida to take over Hindman's Division, relieving Brown. Stewart's command, formerly the Army of Mississippi, was officially redesignated Stewart's Corps, Army of Tennessee. Finally, Hardee, who asked to be reassigned, and whom Hood wanted to replace, remained with the army only after a personal appeal from the president.

Sherman, too, faced organizational changes. Chief among these was selecting a replacement for McPherson. "Black Jack" Logan handled the responsibility of army command admirably in the wake of McPherson's death, but he was a volunteer general, a politician, and significantly, not a West

STEPHEN D. LEE

Born South Carolina 1833; Lee was graduated from the U.S. Military Academy in 1854, seventeenth in his class of forty-six; commissioned a 2d lieutenant in the artillery, he served against the Seminoles in Florida and on the frontier; promoted to 1st lieutenant, he resigned his commission in February 1861, shortly after South Carolina seceded from the Union; appointed a captain in the state's service, he soon entered the Confederate army with the same rank; he was aide-de-camp to General P.G.T. Beauregard at Charleston during the firing upon Fort Sumter; a gifted artillerist, he was also prized as an instructor and administrator; promoted to major in November 1861, he served as an artillery officer during the Peninsular Campaign, Second Manassas, and Sharpsburg; rising through the ranks to brigadier general in November 1862, he was ordered west and performed well during the

Pointer. To Logan's surprise, Sherman selected Fourth Corps commander O.O. Howard for the Army of the Tennessee post. Joe Hooker, Howard's senior, outraged at the appointment, resigned. The command of the Fourth Corps fell to Major General David S. Stanley. To fill Hooker's spot, Sherman summoned Major General Henry Slocum from Vicksburg. Logan, though bitterly disappointed, returned to his corps.

With Atlanta invested on the north and east, Sherman turned his attention to cutting Hood's sole line of supply, the Macon & Western railroad. To this end, he ordered the cavalry divisions of Major General George Stoneman, and Brigadier Generals Edward McCook and Kenner Garrard to strike the rail line leading into Atlanta. In concert with the cavalry raid, Howard's army moved from its position east of the city to the

Vicksburg Campaign of 1863; forced to surrender with the Vicksburg garrison, he was later exchanged and returned to duty with a promotion to major general in August 1863; given charge of all cavalry in the Department of Alabama, Mississippi, and Eastern louisiana, he assumed command of the department in May 1864; in late June he was elevated to lieutenant general and ordered to report to Atlanta to assume command of a corps in General John B. Hood's Army of Tennessee; he initiated the disastrous Battle of Ezra Church and fought poorly at Jonesboro; he led his corps during Hood's Tennessee Campaign and was wounded at Nashville in December 1864; returning to duty in February 1865, he joined General J.E. Johnston's command in North Carolina and surrendered in April; after the war he settled in Mississippi, where he pursued several business interests, served in the state senate, and was president of Mississippi A&M College; he was active in the establishment of the Vicksburg National Military Park and served as its commissioner; during the last years of his life, he was commander-in-chief of the United Confederate Veterans; General Lee died at Vicksburg in 1908; he was the youngest of the Confederacy's lieutenant generals; although talented and well regarded, he was inconsistent in corps command.

extreme right, west of Atlanta, in preparation for a move on the railroad at East Point.

Informed of the Federal movements on July 27, Hood ordered S.D. Lee's and Stewart's Corps to stand ready, and dispatched Wheeler to deal with Sherman's cavalry. The next morning Lee moved to the west to block Howard's intended envelopment. Although Lee was only thirty-one, his Confederate service dated to Fort Sumter. But his experience was in artillery and cavalry; he had had little exposure to infantry or field command. He moved promptly, and by noon was in contact with Howard's pickets, already in position on

GEORGE STONEMAN

Born New York 1822; graduated from the U.S. Military Academy in 1846, thirty-third in his class of fifty-nine that included "Stonewall" Jackson, George B. McClellan, George Pickett, and several other future Civil War generals; posted to dragoons and commissioned 2d lieutenant, he served in California during the Mexican War; promoted to 1st lieutenant, his service was largely in the Southwest; in 1855 he became a captain in the newly-formed elite 2d Cavalry in Texas; he managed to escape capture following the surrender of Texas' military facilities in 1861; promoted to major in the 1st (later 4th) U.S. Cavalry at the outbreak of the Civil War; commissioned brigadier general of volunteers in August 1861; he held a variety of cavalry commands in the Army of the Potomac in the early stages of the war, including a division during the Peninsular Campaign; he led an infantry division at Antietam in September 1862; promoted to major general of volunteers in November, he led a corps at Fredericksburg in December; he then commanded the Cavalry Corps, Army of the Potomac, but his ill-timed and ineffectual raid during the Chancellorsville Campaign in May 1863 left

Lick Skillet Road near Ezra Church west of Atlanta. Hood's overall plan, another from the "Lee and Jackson school," called for Lee to hold Howard in place, while Stewart moved around the Federal flank to strike Howard on the morning of the twenty-ninth. But Lee, believing he had caught Howard off guard, ordered his divisions to form for battle.

As they had the week before, Lee's men faced Lightburn's and Martin's Brigades of Morgan Smith's 2d Division of the Fifteenth Corps . Without waiting for his corps to concentrate, Lee launched Hindman's Division, still commanded by J.C. Brown (Anderson had not yet arrived) in a disjointed attack.

General Joseph Hooker's force open to surprise and defeat; although not at fault, Stoneman was relieved; he then headed the Cavalry Bureau in Washington, D.C., for the remainder of the year; transferred to the Western Theater in January 1864, he commanded briefly the Twenty-third Corps, Army of the Ohio, before assuming direction of that army's cavalry division; he led his division in the Atlanta Campaign but was captured with a large portion of his command during a ill-conceived and poorly executed raid in July 1864; exchanged in October, he took command of the Department of the Ohio and in December led a month-long raid on the salt works and lead mines in southwestern Virginia; in March 1865 he assumed direction of the District of East Tennessee from which he led a highly effective raid into North Carolina in support of General W.T. Sherman's campaign in that state; brevetted through major general in the regular army, he mustered out of the volunteer organization and reverted to his actual rank of lieutenant colonel (since 1863); in the post-war reorganization of the army he became colonel of the 21st Infantry, serving mostly in Arizona until resigning his commission in 1871; settling on his estate near Los Angeles, he served as railroad commissioner and as Democratic governor of California from 1883 to 1887. General Stoneman died at Buffalo, New York, in 1894. He was among the Union's most experienced cavalry officers. Despite his miserable performance in the Atlanta Campaign, Stoneman was essentially a capable soldier.

This time, the Midwesterners quickly repulsed the Rebel advance. Lee then ordered Brigadier General Randall Gibson's Louisiana Brigade from Clayton's Division into the fray, unsupported. Gibson's, one of the best brigades in the army, attacked vigorously but it too was driven back with heavy losses. Clayton's other two brigades advanced only to withdraw in confusion. Finally, Lee committed his reserve, ordering Manigault's Brigade forward. They, too, went unsupported, and after two futile attempts to take a hill on Morgan Smith's front, the men who had done so well the week before retired.

The Battle of Ezra Church
July 28, 1864

Howard had feared such an attack. Despite Sherman's insistence that no attack would be forthcoming, he had prepared for the eventuality. His caution paid off, and Lee's attacks were handled easily. Still, believing Hood to be sending his entire force against him, Howard petitioned Sherman for reinforcements. He also ordered artillery massed on the Fifteenth Corps front, and backed Logan's line with regiments from the Sixteenth and Seventeenth Corps.

Despite his lack of success, Lee believed the opportunity for victory remained. He sent to Stewart, whose corps was moving out as planned, for help in resuming the attack. Stewart agreed, ordering Walthall's Division to Lee's front, followed by Loring's. About 2 P.M. Walthall's force attacked ferociously, but when promised support from Clayton failed to materialize, Walthall disengaged after suffering more than 1,000 casualties. General Walthall also found himself suddenly in command of Stewart's Corps. Riding to the front, Stewart was struck in the head by a spent ball and disabled. Loring, the senior division commander, went down with a leg wound, leaving Walthall to direct both his own and Loring's divisions.

Lee's attack, though well intentioned, had ended in disaster. His casualties neared 3,000, compared to less than 600 in Howard's army. More important, the unplanned battle at Ezra Church effectively canceled the attack planned for the next day. In addition, Hood could ill afford even the temporary loss of Stewart and Loring. When Hood learned of Lee's battle, he immediately dispatched Hardee to direct the action, but by the time he arrived, the damage was done. Hood later sent Cheatham to take control of Stewart's Corps. Lee's ill-advised attack did yield one positive result—it ended Howard's move on East Point and the railroad. But according to Hardee, "no action of the campaign probably did so much to demoralize and dishearten the troops engaged in it." In something of an understatement, Hood reported a "sharp engagement," that ended in "no decided advantage to either side." While he bore ultimate responsibility for the bloody affair, he had not ordered it or wanted it to happen.

Sherman's army had again prevailed in a battle that the general had not expected; yet it was no closer to capturing Atlanta. But, with the cavalry unleashed to the south, the Federals could still cripple Hood's supply line. Stoneman was to move from Decatur and feint to the east before turning south to rendezvous with McCook. McCook would swing west of Atlanta to fall on Lovejoy's Station from that direction. Garrard's role was to decoy Wheeler's horsemen to the southeast and then block their pursuit of Stoneman. Stoneman also had gained permission for a further raid on Macon to liberate Federal officers imprisoned there, and then to Andersonville, where some 30,000 prisoners were held. Sherman expected quick results. By severing Hood's lifeline, Sherman hoped to induce him to abandon Atlanta, or at least force him to come out of the city and fight.

The raid that held so much expectation quickly dissolved into disaster. As the battle raged at Ezra Church, Hood responded to the Federal raid by playing his one discernible advantage—his cavalry. Wheeler's troopers promptly cornered Garrard's force at Flat Rock southeast of Atlanta and drove it northward. Learning of McCook's drive toward Lovejoy's, Wheeler left a brigade to watch Garrard, sent three brigades under Brigadier General Alfred Iverson to find Stoneman, and led the balance of his force to Lovejoy's. On the twenty-ninth McCook reached Lovejoy's after spending the previous day wrecking the Atlanta & West Point line and a supply train at Palmetto. "It was a trail of fire from Palmetto," recalled Lieutenant Granville West of the 4th Kentucky Mounted Infantry, "and the whole heavens were lighted up all night by the flames from burning stores and army equipments." At Lovejoy's, McCook's men devoted themselves to ripping up tracks, tearing down telegraph wires, and destroying supply stocks, but with no sign of Stoneman, and with Rebel cavalry

ALFRED IVERSON

Born Georgia 1829; at the age of seventeen Iverson served as a volunteer officer during the Mexican War; returning to Georgia in 1848, he pursued a variety interests until 1855, when he was commissioned a 1st Lieutenant in the newly constituted 1st U.S. Cavalry; he served on the frontier and in the Mormon Expedition; with the onset of the Civil War, he resigned his commission to enter Confederate service as a captain in March 1861; assigned to North Carolina, he recruited and became colonel of the 20th North Carolina Infantry; he led the regiment to Virginia and was wounded during the Seven Days' Battles; returning to duty he served at South Mountain and Sharpsburg, where he assumed command of the brigade on the death of General Samuel Garland; promoted to brigadier general in November 1862, Iverson led his brigade at Fredericksburg that December and at Chancellorsville the following spring; at Gettysburg his brigade was severely mauled and Iverson apparently lost his nerve; banished from the Army of Northern Virginia, he returned to Georgia, where he assumed command of state troops at Rome; given a cavalry brigade in General Joseph Wheeler's corps during the Atlanta Campaign, Iverson  redeemed himself when his brigade destroyed General George Stoneman's Federal division near Macon in July 1864, capturing Stoneman and more than five hundred of his troopers; Iverson led his brigade for the remainder of the war, surrendering in April 1865; after the war he engaged in business in Georgia before moving to Florida, where he became an orange grower; General Iverson died at Atlanta in 1911; his rout of Stoneman was one of the most lopsided cavalry victories of the war.

closing in, McCook started his division northward. Just west of Lovejoy's, McCook's column ran into Brigadier General William "Red" Jackson's Confederate cavalry and cut to the southwest. Wheeler's force joined Jackson's pursuit and, after an all-night running battle, trapped McCook's exhausted troopers near Newnan. McCook told his men to cut their way out as best they could. Most, including McCook, succeeded, returning piecemeal to the safety of the Union lines. Lieutenant West and what was left of his regiment came in on August 3 "as exhausted as men and horses could well be, and still be able to move." Wheeler proudly reported to Hood, "We have just completed the killing, capturing, and breaking up of the entire raiding party under General McCook."

Stoneman, who had no intention of fulfilling his primary objective, headed straight for Macon, which he reached on the thirtieth. After a feeble attempt to seize the town, he disengaged, abandoning his noble but unrealistic effort. As his command moved northward toward Decatur, they found their path blocked by Iverson's troopers. Following hours of skirmishing, Iverson closed his trap. Parts of Stoneman's command escaped, but he and 700 of his men surrendered. Iverson, in reporting Stoneman's surrender, noted that "the rest of his command is scattered and flying. . . . Many have been already killed and captured." Stoneman's personal goal had been to restore a reputation lost earlier in the war in Virginia. He was now a prisoner of war. Not until August 7 did the final remnants of McCook's and Stoneman's Divisions reach the Federal lines. The Great Raid, of which Sherman expected so much, had ended in the destruction of two cavalry divisions. What damage McCook had managed was quickly repaired.

As July came to a close, Atlanta remained very much in Confederate hands. In his first two weeks of command, Hood had fought three major battles, beaten back two serious efforts to sever his southside rail communications, and held

Sherman's armies in substantially the same place as he had found them on July 18.

For Sherman, on the other hand, the urgency to capture Atlanta was growing daily. As August arrived, neither he nor Grant, in Virginia, had been able to give Lincoln the kind of victory that would galvanize public support. To the contrary, Grant's bloody campaign against Robert E. Lee had only heightened antiwar sentiment in the North. While Sherman had accomplished much, he had not destroyed the Rebel army, and he had not captured Atlanta. With the November election looming, time was running out. If Atlanta was to be taken, it had to be soon.

Two weeks of intense fighting and constant contact in the sweltering Georgia heat left both sides worn down. Hood had suffered more than 12,000 casualties in his unsuccessful bid to inflict a decisive defeat on the Federals. Sherman's losses, although substantially less than Hood's, were heavy, and weeks of ceaseless campaigning had taken a toll. Still, neither side showed any intention of yielding. As Hood awaited the next Federal movement, Sherman prepared the grand stroke that he hoped would deliver Atlanta into his hands.

7

ATLANTA IS OURS

On August 4 Sherman made the first move, renewing his bid to force Hood out of Atlanta. He directed Schofield's single-corps army, which had moved to the extreme right (west of Atlanta), to seize the Macon line between Atlanta and East Point. Sherman also attached John Palmer's Fourteenth Corps to the attack column. But Palmer refused to be placed under Schofield's orders—an act that resulted in confusion, a loss of valuable time, and the departure of Palmer from the army. By nightfall on the fifth, Schofield's command occupied a position between the north and south forks of Utoy Creek, some six miles west of Atlanta. Following the sluggish performance of the Fourteenth Corps during the day's advance, Schofield put his own divisions, those of Brigadier Generals Jacob Cox and Milo Hascall, in the lead.

The next morning, Cox advanced, driving in Rebel pickets. But his attack, spearheaded by Colonel John Reilly's Brigade, soon confronted a series of obstructions backed by Bate's Division from Hardee's Corps. Bate, deployed on the left of Lee's Corps to extend the Rebel line southwestward, easily repulsed Cox's effort. Hascall then swung right in an attempt to hit Bate in the flank. Only the dismounted troopers of Brigadier General L.S. "Sul" Ross's Texas Brigade and a two-gun battery stood in his way. Although Hascall's men actually carried the position, they ran out of time. Darkness soon ended the encounter.

On August 7 Schofield found his path to East Point blocked by increasingly formidable Rebel works. Thus, frustrated in yet another attempt, Sherman wired Chief of Staff Major General Henry Halleck: "I am too impatient for a siege, but I do not know but here is as good a place to fight it out as farther inland. One thing is certain, whether we get inside Atlanta or not, it will be a used-up community by the time we are through with it." He determined "to make the inside of Atlanta too hot to be endured."

Sporadic Federal artillery fire had been striking the city since it first came within range. Most of Atlanta's buildings had been damaged and others leveled, but the bombardment had done little to disrupt military operations. As many as 5,000 citizens remained in Atlanta, enduring the shelling in cellars, caves, and makeshift bomb shelters. On August 9 the bombardment suddenly and dramatically intensified as some 3000 rounds pounded the city, initiating a more or less continuous barrage that would last two weeks. Although reports of hundreds of civilian deaths were widely circulated, the actual number probably did not exceed thirty. Atlantans adjusted to their new routine, and the bombardment brought Sherman no closer to his prize.

Meanwhile, emboldened by the success of his cavalry, and unable to drive Sherman from Atlanta by force, Hood determined to use Wheeler's troopers to further advantage. "Wheeler and Iverson having thus thoroughly crippled the

Federal cavalry," Hood later wrote, "I determined to detach all the troops of that arm I could possibly spare, and expedite them, under the command of Wheeler, against Sherman's railroad to Nashville." He wired the president on August 2: "I hope now to be able, by interrupting Sherman's communications, either to force him to fight me in position or to retreat." Davis concurred with the plan, and added a bit of advice. "The loss consequent upon attacking him [Sherman] in his entrenchments," he cautioned his young general, "requires you to avoid that if practicable." Nothing in this cautionary note indicated Davis's displeasure with Hood's performance to this point, but rather confirmed the course of action that Hood proposed.

Thus, while Sherman reluctantly began siege operations, including the persistent bombardment of Atlanta, Hood unleashed Joe Wheeler on Sherman's rail lifeline. The young cavalryman set out on August 10 with three divisions of cavalry—about 4,500 troopers in all—with orders to wreck the Western & Atlantic between Marietta and Dalton, then move into Tennessee, to destroy as much of the Nashville line as possible. His horsemen struck the railroad at numerous places, but inflicted only moderate damage. By August 14 Wheeler's raid reached Dalton, but rather than moving on the line between Chattanooga and Nashville, Wheeler inexplicably headed into East Tennessee. This change of plan effectively removed Wheeler and the bulk of his cavalry from the campaign. He would not rejoin Hood until long after the struggle for Atlanta was decided. The damage that the Rebel troopers inflicted on Sherman's supply and communications lines was readily repaired. Also, Hood now had only "Red" Jackson's already overworked division at his disposal.

Wheeler's raid soon proved more detrimental to Hood than to Sherman, for on learning of it, the Federal commander decided to exploit the absence of the dreaded Rebel cavalry. Sherman postponed a plan to move with the bulk of his force on a "circle of desolation around Atlanta" in favor of giving his

HUGH JUDSON KILPATRICK

Born New Jersey 1836; Kilpatrick was graduated from the U.S. Military Academy with the May class of 1861, ranking seventeenth of forty-five cadets; although commissioned a 2d lieutenant in the regular army he accepted a volunteer commission as captain in the 5th New York Infantry; he was wounded in the action at Big Bethel in June 1861; returning to duty, he became lieutenant colonel of the 2d New York Cavalry; after a brief assignment in Kansas, he returned to the Eastern Theater, where he participated in numerous actions; promoted to colonel in December 1862, he led a cavalry brigade of the Army of the Potomac in General George Stoneman's raid on Richmond and at Beverly Ford; promoted to brigadier general, U.S. Volunteers, he commanded a division at Gettysburg and Brandy Station; in February 1864 he led the celebrated but disastrous Kilpatrick-Dahlgren Raid on Richmond; transferred to the West, he commanded a cavalry division during the Atlanta Campaign; badly wounded at Resaca in May 1864, he returned to lead a large but unsuccessful raid to cut the railroad south of Atlanta; he commanded the cavalry during General W.T. Sherman's March to the Sea and the Carolinas Campaign; promoted to major general of volunteers in June 1865, he was also breveted through major

general in the regular army; he resigned both his regular and volunteer commissions to become U.S. minister to Chile, where he served until 1868; after an unsuccessful political career, he was reappointed minister to Chile in 1881; he died at Santiago that same year. A spirited fighter, Kilpatrick was also a notorious lady's man and often exercised poor judgement in both arenas; his reckless campaigning led his men to call him "Kil-Cavalry."

cavalry one more shot at Hood's southside railroad. For the task, he selected Brigadier General Judson Kilpatrick, whose division had been brought up to replace the wrecked commands of Stoneman and McCook. Reinforced by two brigades from Kenner Garrard's Division, Kilpatrick's column of close to 5,000 men left the Federal lines west of Atlanta at dusk on August 18, headed for Jonesboro, some fifteen miles south of the city. Only Ross's tiny brigade stood between the Yankee horsemen and Jonesboro.

Although outnumbered better than ten to one, the Texans managed to slow the advance. Kilpatrick's raiders did not reach Jonesboro until late afternoon on the nineteenth. After wrecking rails and destroying stores, the Federal troopers moved late at night toward Lovejoy's Station just south of Jonesboro. But before they could resume their destruction the next day, they were confronted by two brigades of "Red" Jackson's cavalry and a brigade of infantry. Kilpatrick's command successfully fought their way out of the trap and returned to the Federal lines on the twenty-second. The raid, as with all cavalry raids during the campaign, did little lasting damage. By the time the weary troopers reached Decatur, Rebel trains were rolling again into Atlanta.

Sherman had not wanted a siege and still refused to attack the Rebels in place. But Hood had checked every move on his southside communications and would not abandon them as long as supplies were reaching the city. "I became," Sherman recalled, "more than ever convinced that cavalry could not or would not work hard enough to disable a railroad properly, and therefore resolved at once to proceed to the execution of my original plan." He would leave one corps to guard his rear areas and move with the balance of his force far around the Confederate left to strike the railroad south of the city.

Accordingly, on August 25 the month-long bombardment suddenly ceased. Thomas pulled his Army of the Cumberland out of its lines north and east of Atlanta and deployed Slocum's

Twentieth Corps to guard the Chattahoochee bridge and the railroad. Stanley's Fourth Corps moved to the west side to join the rest of Sherman's forces for the move on Jonesboro. Taking great pains to disguise their movements, the Federal columns pressed forward, expecting a Confederate challenge that did not come, as Sherman assumed, because the Rebels believed the Federals were in retreat. On the twenty-eighth Howard's and Thomas's men cut the West Point railroad, and devoted the entire next day to its total destruction. By August 30, Howard's command stood within striking distance of Jonesboro.

Jacob Cox wrote that Hood had "jumped at the conclusion...that Sherman was retreating across the Chattahoochie." This information, supplied by Hardee long after the fact, became the prevailing version of events. If, in fact, Hood was under such an illusion, it was short lived. On the morning of August 26 Hood began a series of orders, directing his army to stand ready. The next morning Hood informed Richmond that the Federals appeared to be moving to their right—west of the city—and that "They have no troops nearer than four miles of Atlanta." Unsure of Sherman's intentions, Hood had little choice but to await his adversary's next move. By the twenty-eighth, based on reports from his cavalry, Hood recalled, "it became at once evident that Sherman was moving with his main body to destroy the Macon road." But these days of ignorance and indecision proved fatal; by the time Hood discovered Sherman's intention it was already too late.

During the evening of the thirtieth Hood countered the Federal thrust by ordering Hardee's and Lee's corps to Jonesboro, with Hardee exercising overall command. That night, during a conference at Hood's headquarters, he "impressed upon General Hardee," the commanding general recalled, "that the fate of Atlanta rested upon his ability, with the aid of two corps, to drive the Federals across Flint River, at Jonesboro." Hood directed Hardee to attack the following morning, and reinforced the urgency of the situation in repeated telegrams throughout the night and into the morning. At 10:00 A.M. on August 31 Hardee received a final admonition to attack "with bayonets fixed, determined to drive everything they may come against."

After a series of delays, it was not until 2:00 P.M. that Hardee had his force deployed for the assault on Howard's army. The two Confederate corps faced westward, with Hardee's, commanded by Pat Cleburne, on the left and Lee's on the right. Hardee planned an *en echelon* advance by brigades from left to right. At 3 P.M. Rebel artillery opened, signalling the beginning of battle. The divisions of Hardee's Corps

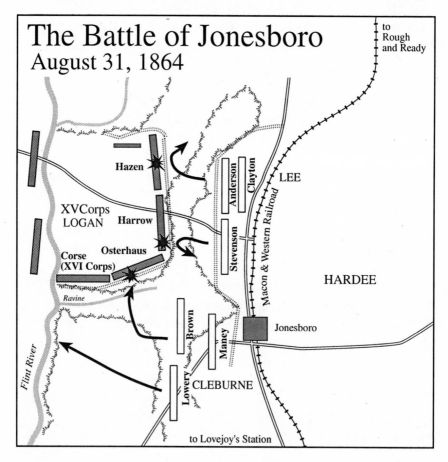

The Battle of Jonesboro
August 31, 1864

attacked with little effect, and were repulsed handily by "Black Jack" Logan's entrenched Fifteenth Corps veterans. Mistaking skirmish fire from Cleburne's front as the beginning of the general advance, Lee, not waiting for the prescribed development, ordered his men forward only to see them cut to pieces by fire from the well-fortified Federal position. General Randall Gibson seized the colors of one of his Louisiana regiments and led his brigade to the Federal works before being driven back with 50 percent casualties. Patton Anderson, having relieved Brown at the head of Hindman's old division, was shot through the jaw while urging his men forward. With little fight left in either corps, Hardee suspended the attack after less than two hours, having incurred more than 2,000 casualties and inflicted less than 200. The first Battle of Jonesboro was over.

Of the bungled attacks, General Manigault recalled sarcastically:

> Major General Anderson, commanding the division, rode up with an aide, apparently much excited, and ordered me to advance and attack again. As he rode along the line, he addressed the troops, and urged them on. It certainly was an act of consummate generalship to push forward 7 or 800 men, just defeated, of scattered commands, no other troops to support them within 500 yards, against I do not know how many thousands. The result was as might have been expected. The folly of the order was so evident to all that nothing but the habit of obedience to the orders of their superior officers, carried them forward for a space, but as soon as they again got well under fire, they broke easily, and fell back to the last position.

Manigault also noted the marked absence of fighting elan among his troops: "I never saw our men fight with so little spirit as at Jonesboro." Manigault's statement notwithstanding, several units attacked with alacrity. The rushed deployment to Jonesboro and a critical shortage of experienced officers no doubt hampered the Rebels' performance. But nothing so demoralized the troops as attacking a well-entrenched enemy of plainly superior number and firepower. One Federal colonel reported that his 200-man regiment expended 19,000 rounds of ammunition during the day.

Hood described the effort as "feeble," and, with a few notable exceptions, accounts supported the general's opinion. But even the most spirited attack had little chance of success. Still, Hardee's plan virtually assured failure. He ordered an attack that he did not believe could succeed and simply sent his troops forward as ordered. The *en echelon* advance, bungled from the start, did not allow a concentrated thrust, accounting for a piecemeal attack. Although Howard had his entire army and most of Thomas's at his disposal, he required only a single corps to repel Hardee's attack. Disgusted by the fact that the attack was not delivered in the spirit that the emergency demanded, Hood again looked to casualty figures to confirm his belief. But Hood no longer confined his wrath to Johnston or Hardee; he did the unthinkable, citing the "disgraceful effort...made by our men" in reference to the day's casualties. The critical nature of the moment and the pressures of command notwithstanding, Hood's sanguinary method of analysis did much to foster his reputation as a butcher.

While the battle raged to the south, Jacob Cox's Division of Schofield's Twenty-third Corps cut the Macon railroad at Rough and Ready between Atlanta and Jonesboro. Soon Schofield's other division, Milo Hascall's, and Stanley's Fourth Corps from Thomas's army joined Cox's men in wrecking the railroad and telegraph. Not only had Sherman's army finally severed Hood's only lifeline, but it now stood between Hardee's command and the balance of Hood's army in Atlanta. As August came to a close, Sherman's campaign reached its climax. The prize was his for the taking.

In Atlanta, Hood could only wait for word from Hardee. Reports of Yankee troop movements indicated a major move was imminent. But Hood, who had no telegraph communication with Jonesboro, believed a major attack would fall on Atlanta. He dispatched couriers with orders directing Hardee to return Lee's Corps to the city and to protect the approach to Macon. Not until midnight on September 1 did Hardee receive the order and, while he could ill afford to do so, "Old Reliable" ordered Lee northward. The veteran then prepared for the defense of Jonesboro and the Macon railroad southward. After midnight, Hood finally received word of the debacle at Jonesboro and the Federal occupation of his railroad near Rough and Ready. Facing the prospect of being trapped, and recognizing that his army could not stand a siege for long, Hood that morning ordered the evacuation of Atlanta.

Preparations for the evacuation and retreat commenced immediately. Lee's Corps, returning from Jonesboro, was stopped east of Rough and Ready to cover the sole Confederate escape route—the McDonough Road that led southeastward from the city. Hood would then move his army out the McDonough Road and attempt a rendezvous with Hardee south of Jonesboro.

At Jonesboro, Hardee's single corps faced Howard's three on roughly the same front as the day before. Owing to massive attrition, replacements commanded most of Hardee's divisions and brigades. The approach of the Fourteenth Corps from the Army of the Cumberland forced Hardee to refuse his right flank, creating a dangerous salient manned by three of the army's best brigades. Daniel Govan's Arkansans, backed by two batteries, held the point, with Brigadier General Hiram Granbury's Texas Brigade to the left and Brigadier General Joseph Lewis's Kentucky "Orphan Brigade" on the right. The arrival of yet another Federal force, Stanley's Fourth Corps, on his right flank prompted Hardee to further adjust his line, creating a rough inverted "V". Hardee's veteran corps had fought with mixed effect throughout the campaign, but now, as it had following the disaster at Missionary Ridge, it would be fighting for the very existence of the army.

At 4 P.M. on September 1 the second battle for Jonesboro began as Brevet Major General Jefferson C. Davis, the new commander of the Fourteenth Corps, threw his men against Hardee's vulnerable salient. The first assault made headway but, hampered by a variety of obstructions, pulled up short of

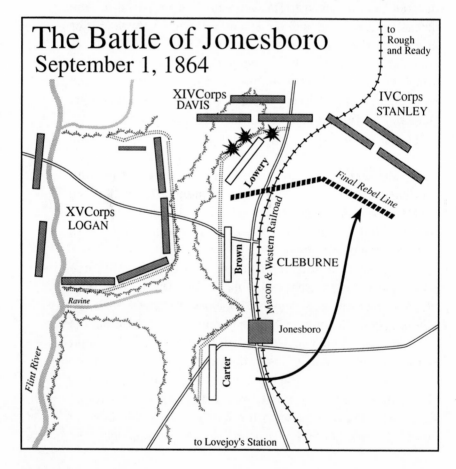

The Battle of Jonesboro
September 1, 1864

to Rough and Ready

XIVCorps
DAVIS

IVCorps
STANLEY

Lowery

Final Rebel Line

XVCorps
LOGAN

Brown

Macon & Western Railroad

CLEBURNE

Ravine

Flint River

Jonesboro

Carter

to Lovejoy's Station

the Rebel works. At 5 P.M. Davis resumed the assault with added weight. The furious advance pierced Cleburne's line, despite the herculean resistance from Govan's and Lewis's Brigades. The Federals soon overwhelmed the salient, capturing Govan, most of his brigade, and two Rebel batteries. "It came in an instant upon Govan," observed Colonel Charles Olmstead of the 1st Georgia, "the attacking column rising suddenly from the valley, rank after rank, had but a short rush to make and literally ran over his slender line." A desperate counterattack directed by Cleburne stemmed the Federal breakthrough, but the damage was done. Fortunately for the Confederates, General Davis, content with his achievement, and with darkness falling, ended the assault.

Although successful, Davis's attack netted little in terms of meaningful results. Hardee's Corps, while severely battered, still held the railroad. Throughout the battle, Howard's entire army stood dormant, and, to Sherman's intense displeasure, the Fourth Corps never meaningfully engaged. The Federals missed an extraordinary opportunity to destroy Hardee's Corps and gain control of the Macon road.

As Hardee prepared for Davis's final onslaught at Jonesboro, the remainder of Hood's army began its evacuation of Atlanta. Before midnight the Confederate rear guard, Major General Samuel French's Division from Stewart's Corps and Brigadier General Samuel Ferguson's cavalry Brigade, followed their comrades out of the city. Before leaving, the Rebels torched two large munitions trains and other valuable stores trapped in Atlanta, as Hood reported, "owing to the wanton neglect of the chief quartermaster." The monumental explosion that followed, more than anything else, signalled the fall of Atlanta.

That night, Hardee managed to slip out of Jonesboro undetected, reaching Lovejoy's early on September 2 after an all night march that Colonel Olmstead described as a "horrible dream." As he recalled, "the red glare in the northern sky and the sullen rumble of distant explosions told that Hood was burning his stores and abandoning Atlanta to Sherman." The struggle for Atlanta had come to an end.

As Hardee's men dug in at Lovejoy's, and while Hood with Stewart's and Lee's Corps moved to join them, the mayor of Atlanta surrendered the city to troops from Henry Slocum's advancing Twentieth Corps. Sherman, unaware of the events in Atlanta and furious that Hardee had escaped, led the bulk of his army toward Lovejoy's. While the Union commander was feeling Hardee's position, confirmation of Hood's evacuation of Atlanta and the city's subsequent surrender reached him. "So Atlanta is ours, and fairly won," he wired Halleck on September 3, "I shall not push much farther on this raid, but in a day or so will move to Atlanta and give my men some rest."

Hood managed to consolidate his depleted army at Lovejoy's, where it remained unmolested for three weeks. In

JEFFERSON C. DAVIS

Born Indiana 1828; Davis fought in the Mexican War as a teen-aged volunteer; commissioned into the regular army as 2d lieutenant of artillery in 1848, gaining promotion to 1st lieutenant in 1852; he was on duty during the bombardment of Fort Sumter in April 1861; promoted to captain in May, Davis entered the volunteer army in August as colonel of the 22d Indiana Infantry, with which he fought at Wilson's Creek, Missouri; promoted to brigadier general, U.S. Volunteers, to rank from December, he led a division at Pea Ridge, Arkansas, in March 1862 and at Corinth, Mississippi; in September 1862 at Louisville, Kentucky, Davis initiated an altercation with his superior, General William "Bull" Nelson, in which Davis shot and killed Nelson,

late September, Hood moved north to threaten Sherman's supply line between Atlanta and Chattanooga, striking the
Western & Atlantic at many familiar points. Hood's advance
reached as far north as Dalton before veering west into the
fastness of northern Alabama. The hit-and-run campaign kept
Sherman's army busy in north Georgia for a full two months
after the fall of Atlanta.

In early November President Abraham Lincoln won reelection, thanks in large part to Sherman's victory in Georgia. Shortly
thereafter Sherman finally received Grant's permission to press
on southward. After detailing Thomas with Schofield's army and
part of the Army of the Cumberland to deal with Hood, Sherman
commenced his "March to the Sea." Hood went on to invade
western Tennessee, only to meet with disaster at Franklin and
Nashville. The names Sherman and Hood henceforth became
synonymous with Union victory and Confederate defeat.

reportedly in cold blood; no charges were ever filed and Davis returned to duty,
commanding a division in the Army of the Cumberland at Stone's River,
Chickamauga, and during the Atlanta Campaign; in August 1864 he assumed
command of the Fourteenth Corps, with the brevet rank of major general, U.S.
Volunteers; he led the corps with distinction for the remainder of the Atlanta
Campaign, in General William T. Sherman's March to the Sea, and in the
Carolinas Campaign of 1865; brevetted through major general, U.S. Army,
Davis never received promotion to the full rank of major general of volunteers,
for which he was entitled and repeatedly recommended; although embittered
by this perceived injustice, he continued in the regular army as colonel of the
23d Infantry, exercising departmental command in Alaska and participating in
the campaign against the Modoc Indians in California; General Davis died at
Chicago in 1879. Although his killing of General Nelson doubtless affected his
promotion and likely prevented a more prominent role in the post-war army,
Davis was a competent and often outstanding officer.

CONCLUSION
SO STRANGELY
MISREPRESENTED

With the publication of his *Narrative of Military Operations* in 1874, Johnston fired the first volley in what became a sad literary war. He asserted that, at the time of his removal, he was preparing to "engage the enemy," and that if unsuccessful he still could have held Atlanta "forever." He labeled Hood's operations "disastrous," and alluded to the "slaughter" to which the army was "recklessly offered in the four attacks on the Federal army near Atlanta." The general's popularity assured wide acceptance of his version of events. Jacob Cox, for example, in his history of the Atlanta Campaign, bought heavily into Johnston's account. Thus Johnston's became the prevailing interpretation.

Hood took up the challenge and began work on his reply.

"I would have left the work of vindication to the unbiased historian of the future," he wrote, "had not my words and actions been so strangely misrepresented." Hood died in 1879, before he could find a publisher for his book. General P.G.T. Beauregard arranged for the book's publication in the hope of providing some support for Hood's orphaned children. In 1880 Hood's tedious and often pathetic self-defense, *Advance and Retreat*, appeared in print.

Both works reflected poorly on the authors, who justified their wartime efforts at the expense of others and, too often, the truth. Neither man could content himself with the knowledge that he had done the best job that he could do and had served his country faithfully. Hood would have benefitted from such an admission—at least in the eyes of historians. But the times dictated otherwise. Personal honor demanded a duel—if not with pistols then with the pen—that left both participants seriously wounded.

Of the two, Hood's book is better supported by the facts. Joe Johnston conducted a masterful strategic defensive and may well have been correct in his conduct, but this is beside the point. He failed to understand the symbolic or substantive importance of Atlanta and, most important, he refused to act as his government directed. Though he blamed Davis for his ouster, he bore the brunt of the responsibility. Hood's role in Johnston's demise was minimal; although his correspondence with Richmond lacked veracity, it had little, if any, effect on Davis's decision to remove Johnston, or on his own ascension to command.

Any assertion that Hood came to Georgia with a premeditated agenda to gain command of the army is without merit. He no doubt envisioned a large role for himself—playing Stonewall Jackson to Johnston's Lee—and most certainly expected to undertake a bold offensive. When it became evident that no such operation was in the offing, his reaction was inappropriate but understandable. Once given command of the army he inherited a near hopeless situation. Despite the fact that it was Johnston's retreat that had brought Sherman's forces to the outskirts of Atlanta, blame for the campaign's failure fell mostly on Hood. Yet his attacks around Atlanta, although costly, were hardly reckless, and compared to Shiloh, Antietam, Gettysburg, Chickamauga, or the Wilderness could scarcely be considered slaughters. Hood was placed in command to fight; his mandate left him little alternative. His strategy, based largely on Robert E. Lee's Virginia campaigns, was conceptually sound. Hood's failure came in trying to do too much with too little. Also, his physical limitations demanded that he rely heavily on subordinates to direct battles. Still, he managed to keep Sherman out of Atlanta for forty-three days, then effectively occupied him for two months after the city's fall. In commenting on the Johnston-Hood controversy, Federal General Frank Blair concluded that "It was natural enough that after the failure of General Johnston to check our advance, other tactics should be employed; and no man could have been found who could have executed this policy with greater skill, ability, and vigor than General Hood."

To his discredit, Hood placed much of the blame for the failures around Atlanta on his army. Most of Hood's wrath fell on Hardee, who made no secret of his resentment of Hood. But defeat owed more to unrealistic expectations and a lack of manpower than to any failing on the part of Hardee, or Hood for that matter. The shortage of experience at corps and division command levels seriously hampered Hood's army, as evidenced by S.D. Lee's performance and the problems that plagued Cheatham's Corps during the Battle of Atlanta.

William J. Hardee finally received his long-desired transfer from Hood's army but found his next assignment no easier. He commanded troops in the futile opposition of Sherman's March to the Sea and later fought under Johnston in the Carolinas. After the war "Old Reliable" became a planter in Alabama and largely evaded the battle of words between his two former commanders. He died during a visit to Wytheville, Virginia, on November 6, 1873, with his reputation as one of the

Confederacy's best generals very much intact.

Joe Johnston gained a measure of satisfaction when, after Hood's disastrous Tennessee Campaign, he returned to command what was left of the Army of Tennessee in the closing stages of the war. He surrendered his army to Sherman in April 1865. Despite his largely unimpressive war record, he remained extremely popular and, like Sherman, was hailed a master strategist. For Johnston, the Atlanta Campaign never ended. He spent most of his remaining years defending his conduct while vilifying Davis and Hood. Johnston died at Washington, D.C., on March 21, 1891, the result of a cold that he reportedly contracted while attending Sherman's funeral the previous month.

William Tecumseh Sherman entered the Atlanta Campaign largely unproven and emerged a national hero. His subsequent march of devastation through Georgia and the Carolinas became one of the most remembered and, in the South, condemned episodes of the Civil War. Often touted as the first modern general, Sherman followed Grant as commanding general of the United States Army—becoming only the second man in the nation's history to wear four stars. He died at New York City on February 14, 1891.

As Sherman marched to sea and glory, Hood went on to disgrace. His Tennessee Campaign, that ended with the virtual destruction of his army, more than anything else determined how Hood would be judged, and affected negatively the evaluation of his efforts around Atlanta. Relieved at his own request in January 1865, Hood travelled to Richmond, where he secured an ambiguous assignment to Texas. In the meantime, his report on the Atlanta Campaign, largely a scathing indictment of Johnston and Hardee, surfaced. Johnston sought charges against Hood, but the war ended before any action could be taken.

En route to Texas Hood stopped in South Carolina to visit Buck Preston only to learn that her family's objections had prevailed. Crippled, disgraced, and now rejected, Hood continued on to Texas. Before he reached his adopted state, the conflict ended. He surrendered to Federal authorities at Natchez, Mississippi, on the last day of May 1865. After the war Hood settled in New Orleans, becoming first a cotton factor and commission merchant and then an insurance executive.

In April 1868 he married Anna Marie Hennen, the daughter of a prominent Louisiana attorney. In ten years the Hoods had eleven children, eight girls and three boys, including three sets of twins. But a yellow fever epidemic in 1878 devastated Hood's business and, the following year, a subsequent outbreak struck New Orleans. Mrs. Hood contracted the fever and died on August 24, 1879, and was followed two days later by her eldest child Lydia. On August 30, at forty-eight years of age, the general succumbed to the disease.

The Civil War offered an extraordinary opportunity for hundreds of men to command large troop formations in battle, something most had no experience in doing. Those who excelled—and survived—usually earned promotion and greater responsibility. Hood took full advantage of his opportunities, becoming one of the war's most effective combat commanders. But he, like most of the men who rose to command major armies during the war, was elevated to a position that stretched his abilities.

For Hood, the war comprised two almost indistinguishable phases: The first featured glory and rapid advancement fueled by audacious battlefield performances; the second was characterized by wounds, ambition, and ultimate failure. No Civil War officer enjoyed such a meteoric rise or suffered a more catastrophic fall.

APPENDIX A

ORDER OF BATTLE FOR CONFEDERATE FORCES DURING THE ATLANTA CAMPAIGN

THE ARMY OF TENNESSEE
GEN. JOSEPH E. JOHNSTON
GEN. JOHN B. HOOD (*from 18 July*)

CHIEF OF STAFF
BRIG. GEN. WILLIAM W. MACKALL
BRIG. GEN. FRANCIS A. SHOUP (FROM 21 JULY)

CHIEF ENGINEER
LT. COL. STEPHEN W. PRESSTMAN
MAJ. GEN. MARTIN L. SMITH

HARDEE'S CORPS
LT. GEN. WILLIAM J. HARDEE
MAJ. GEN. PATRICK R. CLEBURNE (30 AUGUST–1 SEPTEMBER)

CHEATHAM'S DIVISION
MAJ. GEN. BENJAMIN F. CHEATHAM
BRIG. GEN. GEORGE E. MANEY
BRIG. GEN. JOHN C. CARTER (1 SEPTEMBER)

MANEY'S BRIGADE
BRIG. GEN. GEORGE E. MANEY
COL. GEORGE C. PORTER
COL. FRANCIS M. WALKER
4th Confederate (Tennessee)
1st & 27thTennessee
6th & 9th Tennessee
41st Tennessee
50th Tennessee
24th Tennessee Battalion

WRIGHT'S BRIGADE

Col. John C. Carter

6th Tennessee

8th Tennessee

28th Tennessee

38th Tennessee

51st & 52d Tennessee

STRAHL'S BRIGADE

Brig. Gen. Otho F. Strahl

Col. Andrew J. Kellar

4th & 5th Tennessee

19th Tennessee

24th Tennessee

31st Tennessee

33d Tennessee

41st Tennessee

VAUGHN'S BRIGADE

Brig. Gen. Alfred J. Vaughn (wounded 7 July)

Col. Michael Magevney

Col. George W. Gordon

11th Tennessee

12th & 47th Tennessee

13th & 15th Tennessee

29th Tennessee

CLEBURNE'S DIVISION
Maj. Gen. Patrick R. Cleburne
Brig. Gen. Mark P. Lowrey (30 August–1 September)

POLK'S BRIGADE

(disbanded 24 July)

Brig. Gen. Lucius Polk (wounded 17 June)

1st & 15th Arkansas (to Govan's Brigade)

5th Confederate (to Granbury's Brigade)

2d Tennessee (to Tyler's Brigade)

35th & 48th Tennessee (to Quarles's Brigade)

GOVAN'S BRIGADE

BRIG. GEN. DANIEL C. GOVAN (CAPTURED 1 SEPTEMBER)

2d & 24th Arkansas

5th & 13th Arkansas

6th & 7th Arkansas

8th & 19th Arkansas

3d Confederate

LOWREY'S BRIGADE

BRIG. GEN. MARK P. LOWREY

COL. JOHN WEIR (30 AUGUST–1 SEPTEMBER)

16th Alabama

33d Alabama

45th Alabama

32d Mississippi

45th Mississippi

GRANBURY'S BRIGADE

BRIG. GEN. HIRAM B. GRANBURY

BRIG. GEN. JAMES A. SMITH (WOUNDED 22 JULY)

6th Texas

7th Texas

10th Texas

15th Texas Cavalry (dismounted)

17th & 18th Texas Cavalry (dismounted)

24th & 25th Texas Cavalry (dismounted)

BATE'S DIVISION

MAJ. GEN. WILLIAM F. BATE (WOUNDED 10 AUGUST)

MAJ. GEN. JOHN C. BROWN

TYLER'S (SMITH'S) BRIGADE

BRIG. GEN. THOMAS B. SMITH

4th Georgia Battalion Sharpshooters

37th Georgia

10th Tennessee

15th & 37th Tennessee

20th Tennessee

30th Tennessee

LEWIS'S "ORPHAN" BRIGADE
BRIG. GEN. JOSEPH H. LEWIS
2d Kentucky
4th Kentucky
5th Kentucky
6th Kentucky
9th Kentucky

FINLEY'S BRIGADE
BRIG. GEN. JESSE J. FINLEY (WOUNDED 31 AUGUST)
COL. ROBERT BULLOCK
1st Florida Cavalry (dismounted) & 3d Florida
1st & 4th Florida
6th Florida
7th Florida

WALKER'S DIVISION
(DISBANDED 24 JULY)
MAJ. GEN. W. H. T. WALKER (KILLED 22 JULY)
BRIG. GEN. HUGH MERCER (22–24 JULY)

GIST'S BRIGADE (to Cheatham's Division)
BRIG. GEN. STATES RIGHTS GIST (WOUNDED 22 JULY)
COL. JAMES McCULLOUGH
COL. ELLISON CAPERS
8th Georgia Battalion
46th Georgia
16th South Carolina
24th South Carolina

JACKSON'S BRIGADE (disbanded 1 July)
BRIG. GEN. JOHN K. JACKSON (TO SAVANNAH 1 JULY)
5th Georgia (to Savannah)
47th Georgia (to Savannah)
65th Georgia (to Gist's Brigade)
2d Battalion Georgia Sharpshooters (to Gist's Brigade)
5th Mississippi (to Lowrey's Brigade 24 July)
8th Mississippi (to Lowrey's Brigade 24 July)

STEVENS'S BRIGADE (to Bate's Division)
BRIG. GEN. CLEMENT H. STEVENS (KILLED 20 JULY)
COL. J. COOPER NISBET
BRIG. GEN. HENRY R. JACKSON (FROM 29 JULY)
1st Georgia (Confederate)
25th Georgia
29th Georgia
30th Georgia
66th Georgia
1st Georgia Battalion Sharpshooters

MERCER'S BRIGADE (to Cleburne's Division)
BRIG. GEN. HUGH MERCER (TO SAVANNAH 24 JULY)
COL. CHARLES H. OLMSTEAD
1st Georgia
54th Georgia
57th Georgia
63d Georgia

HOOD'S (LEE'S) CORPS
LT. GEN. JOHN B. HOOD
MAJ. GEN. CARTER L. STEVENSON (18 JULY)
MAJ. GEN. BENJAMIN F. CHEATHAM (19–25 JULY)
LT. GEN. STEPHEN D. LEE (FROM 26 JULY)

HINDMAN'S DIVISION
MAJ. GEN. THOMAS C. HINDMAN (WOUNDED 3 JULY)
BRIG. GEN. JOHN C. BROWN
MAJ. GEN. PATTON ANDERSON (WOUNDED 31 AUGUST)
MAJ. GEN. EDWARD JOHNSON

DEAS'S BRIGADE

BRIG. GEN. ZACHARIAH C. DEAS

COL. JOHN G. COLTART (WOUNDED 28 JULY)

BRIG. GEN. GEORGE D. JOHNSTON (26–28 JULY, WOUNDED 28 JULY)

LT. COL. HARRY T. TOULMIN (28 JULY–6 AUGUST)

19th Alabama

22d Alabama

25th Alabama

39th Alabama

50th Alabama

17th Alabama Battalion Sharpshooters

MANIGUALT'S BRIGADE

BRIG. GEN. ARTHUR M. MANIGAULT

24th Alabama

28th Alabama

34th Alabama

10th South Carolina

19th South Carolina

WALTHALL'S (BRANTLEY'S) BRIGADE

BRIG. GEN. EDWARD C. WALTHALL (TO ARMY OF MISSISSIPPI 6 JUNE)

COL. SAMUEL BENTON (MORTALLY WOUNDED 22 JULY)

COL. (BRIG. GEN.) WILLIAM F. BRANTLEY

24th & 27th Mississippi

29th & 30th Mississippi

34th Mississippi

TUCKER'S (SHARP'S) BRIGADE

BRIG. GEN. WILLIAM F. TUCKER (WOUNDED 14 MAY)

COL. (BRIG. GEN.) JACOB H. SHARP

7th Mississippi

9th Mississippi

10th Mississippi

41st Mississippi

44th Mississippi

9th Mississippi Battalion Sharpshooters

STEVENSON'S DIVISION
MAJ. GEN. CARTER L. STEVENSON

BROWN'S BRIGADE
BRIG. GEN. JOHN C. BROWN
COL. JOSEPH C. PALMER (FROM 11 JULY)
3d Tennessee
18th Tennessee
26th Tennessee
32d Tennessee
45th Tennessee & 23d Tennessee Battalion

CUMMING'S BRIGADE
BRIG. GEN. ALFRED CUMMING (WOUNDED 31 AUGUST)
2d Georgia State Troops
34th Georgia
36th Georgia
39th Georgia
56thGeorgia

REYNOLDS'S BRIGADE
BRIG. GEN. ALEXANDER W. REYNOLDS
58th NorthCarolina
60th NorthCarolina
54th Virginia
63d Virginia

PETTUS'S BRIGADE
BRIG. GEN. EDMUND W. PETTUS
20th Alabama
23d Alabama
30th Alabama
31st Alabama
46th Alabama

STEWART'S (CLAYTON'S) DIVISION
MAJ. GEN. ALEXANDER P. STEWART
MAJ. GEN. HENRY D. CLAYTON (FROM 7 JULY)

STOVALL'S BRIGADE

BRIG. GEN. MARCELLUS A. STOVALL
COL. ABDA JOHNSON (15 MAY–1 JUNE)
COL. ROBERT J. HENDERSON (12–31 AUGUST)

1st Georgia State Troops
40th Georgia
41st Georgia
42d Georgia
43d Georgia
52d Georgia

CLAYTON'S (HOLTZCLAW'S) BRIGADE

BRIG. GEN. HENRY D. CLAYTON
BRIG. GEN. JAMES T. HOLTZCLAW (FROM 10 JULY)
COL. BUSHROD JONES (FROM 22 JULY)

18th Alabama
32d & 58th Alabama
36th Alabama
38th Alabama

GIBSON'S BRIGADE

BRIG. GEN. RANDALL LEE GIBSON

1st Louisiana
4th Louisiana
13th Louisiana
16th & 25th Louisiana
19th Louisiana
20th Louisiana
25th Louisiana
4th Louisiana Battalion
14th Louisiana Battalion Sharpshooters

BAKER'S BRIGADE

BRIG. GEN. ALPHEUS BAKER

37th Alabama
40th Alabama
42d Alabama
54th Alabama

ARMY OF MISSISSIPPI (POLK'S CORPS)
Lt. Gen. Leonidas Polk (killed 14 June)
Maj. Gen. William W. Loring (14 June–7 July)
Maj. Gen. Alexander P. Stewart

STEWART'S CORPS (DESIGNATED 26 JULY)
Lt. Gen. Alexander P. Stewart (wounded 28 July)
Maj. Gen. Benjamin F. Cheatham (temporarily)

LORING'S DIVISION
Maj. Gen. William W. Loring (wounded 28 July)
Brig. Gen. Winfield S. Featherston
(14 June–7 July, from 28 July)

FEATHERSTON'S BRIGADE
Brig. Gen. Winfield S. Featherston
Col. Robert Lowrey (temporarily)
Col. Marcus D. L. Stephens (temporarily)
> 3d Mississippi
> 22d Mississippi
> 31st Mississippi
> 33d Mississippi
> 40th Mississippi
> 1st Mississippi Battalion Sharpshooters

ADAMS'S BRIGADE
Brig. Gen. John Adams
> 6th Mississippi
> 14th Mississippi
> 15th Mississippi
> 20th Mississippi
> 23d Mississippi
> 43d Mississippi

SCOTT'S BRIGADE
Brig. Gen. Thomas M. Scott
> 27th Alabama
> 35th Alabama
> 49th Alabama
> 55th Alabama
> 57th Alabama
> 12th Louisiana

FRENCH'S DIVISION
MAJ. GEN. SAMUEL G. FRENCH

ECTOR'S BRIGADE
BRIG. GEN. MATTHEW D. ECTOR (WOUNDED 27 JULY)
COL. (BRIG. GEN.) WILLIAM H. YOUNG
29th North Carolina
39th North Carolina
9th Texas
10th Texas Cavalry (dismounted)
14th Texas Cavalry (dismounted)
32d Texas Cavalry (dismounted)

COCKRELL'S BRIGADE
BRIG. GEN. FRANCIS M. COCKRELL (WOUNDED 19 JUNE)
COL. ELIJAH GATES (19 JUNE–7 AUGUST)
1st & 4th Missouri
2d & 6th Missouri
3d & 5th Missouri
1st Missouri Cavalry & 3d Missouri Cavalry Battalion
(dismounted)

SEARS'S BRIGADE
BRIG. GEN. CLAUDIUS W. SEARS
COL. WILLIAM S. BARRY (FROM 10 JUNE)
4th Mississippi
35th Mississippi
36th Mississippi
39th Mississippi
46th Mississippi
7th Mississippi Battalion

CANTEY'S (WALTHALL'S) DIVISION
BRIG. GEN. JAMES CANTEY
MAJ. GEN. EDWARD C. WALTHALL (FROM 6 JUNE)

REYNOLDS'S BRIGADE
BRIG. GEN. DANIEL H. REYNOLDS
  1st Arkansas Mounted Rifles (dismounted)
  2d Arkansas Mounted Rifles (dismounted)
  4th Arkansas
  9th Arkansas
  25th Arkansas

CANTEY'S BRIGADE
BRIG. GEN. JAMES CANTEY
COL. EDWARD A. O'NEAL (FROM 27 JUNE)
  17th Alabama
  26th Alabama
  29th Alabama
  37th Mississippi

QUARLES'S BRIGADE
BRIG. GEN. WILLIAM A. QUARLES
  1st Alabama
  4th Louisiana (to Gibson's Brigade)
  30th Louisiana (to Gibson's Brigade)
  42d Tennessee
  46th & 55th Tennessee
  48th Tennessee
  49th Tennessee
  53d Tennessee

CAVALRY CORPS
MAJ. GEN. JOSEPH WHEELER

MARTIN'S DIVISION
MAJ. GEN. WILLIAM T. MARTIN

ALLEN'S BRIGADE
BRIG. GEN. WILLIAM W. ALLEN
  1st Alabama
  3d Alabama
  4th Alabama
  7th Alabama
  51st Alabama
  12th Alabama Battalion

IVERSON'S BRIGADE
Brig. Gen. Alfred Iverson
1st Georgia
2d Georgia
3d Georgia
4th Georgia
6th Georgia

KELLY'S DIVISION
Brig. Gen. John H. Kelly

ANDERSON'S BRIGADE
Brig. Gen. Robert H. Anderson
3d Confederate
8th Confederate
10th Confederate
12th Confederate
5th Georgia

DIBRELL'S BRIGADE
Col. George G. Dibrell
4th Tennessee
8th Tennessee
9th Tennessee
10th Tennessee
11th Tennessee

HANNON'S BRIGADE*
Col. Moses W. Hannon
53d Alabama
24th Alabama Battalion

also reported in Hume's Division

GRIGSBY'S (WILLIAM'S) BRIGADE*
COL. WARREN GRIGSBY
BRIG. GEN. JOHN S. WILLIAMS
1st (3d) Kentucky
2d Kentucky
9th Kentucky
2d Kentucky Battalion
Allison's Tennessee Squadron
Hamilton's Tennessee Battalion

* also reported in Hume's Division

HUME'S DIVISION
BRIG. GEN. WILLIAM Y.C. HUME
1st (6th) Tennessee
2d Tennessee
5th Tennessee
9th Tennessee Batalion

HARRISON'S BRIGADE
COL. THOMAS HARRISON
3d Arkansas
4th Tennessee
8th Texas
11th Texas

JACKSON'S INDEPENDENT DIVISION
(FROM ARMY OF MISSISSIPPI)
BRIG. GEN. WILLIAM H. JACKSON

ARMSTRONG'S BRIGADE
BRIG. GEN. FRANK C. ARMSTRONG
1st Mississippi
2d Mississippi
28th Mississippi
Ballentine's Mississippi Regiment

ROSS'S BRIGADE
Brig. Gen. Lawrence S. Ross
1st Texas Legion
3d Texas
6th Texas
9th Texas

FERGUSON'S BRIGADE
Brig. Gen. Samuel W. Ferguson
2d Alabama
56th Alabama
9th Mississippi
11th Mississippi
12th Mississippi Battalion

ARTILLERY
Brig. Gen. Francis A. Shoup
Col. Robert F. Beckham (from 21 July)

HARDEE'S CORPS
Col. Melancthon Smith

HOXTON'S BATTALION
Maj. Llewelyn Hoxton
Marion (Florida) Light Artillery
Mississippi Battery
Phelan's Alabama Battery

HOTCHKISS'S BATTALION
Maj. Thomas R. Hotchkiss (wounded 21 July)
Capt. Thomas J. Key
Alabama Battery
Key's Arkansas Battery
Warren (Mississippi) Light Artillery

MARTIN'S BATTALION
Maj. Robert Martin
Ferguson's South Carolina Battery
Georgia Battery
Missouri Battery

COBB'S BATTALION
MAJ. ROBERT COBB
Gracey's Kentucky Battery
Mebane's Tennessee Battery
Washington (Louisiana) Light Artillery, 5th Co.

PALMER'S BATTALION
MAJ. JOSEPH PALMER
Alabama Battery
Georgia Battery
Georgia Battery

HOOD'S CORPS
COL. ROBERT F. BECKHAM
LT. COL. JAMES H. HALLONQUIST (FROM 21 JULY)

COURTNEY'S BATTALION
MAJ. ALFRED R. COURTNEY
Dent's Alabama Battery
Garrity's Alabama Battery
Douglas's Texas Battery

ELDRIDGE'S BATTALION
MAJ. JOHN W. ELDRIDGE
Eufaula (Alabama) Artillery
Fenner's Louisiana Battery
Stanford's Mississippi Battery

JOHNSTON'S BATTALION
MAJ. JOHN W. JOHNSTON (WOUNDED 14 MAY)
CAPT. MAXIMILLIAN VAN DEN CORPUT
CAPT. JOHN B. ROWAN
Cherokee (Georgia) Artillery
Stephens (Georgia) Light Artillery
Marshall's Tennessee Battery

WILLIAMS'S BATTALION
LT. COL. SAMUEL C. WILLIAMS
CAPT. REUBEN F. KOLB (FROM 31 JULY)
Barbour (Alabama) Artillery
Jefferson (Mississippi) Artillery
Nottoway (Virginia) Artillery

POLK'S (STEWART'S) CORPS
(ORGANIZED 23 JULY)
LT. COL. SAMUEL C. WILLIAMS

MYRICK'S BATTALION
MAJ. JOHN D. MYRICK
Cowan's Mississippi Battery
Bouanchaud's Louisiana Battery
Barry's Tennessee Battery

STORRS'S BATTALION
MAJ. GEORGE S. STORRS
Guibor's Louisiana Battery
Hoskins's Mississippi Battery
Ward's Alabama Battery

PRESTON'S BATTALION
MAJ. WILLIAM C. PRESTON (KILLED 20 JULY)
MAJ. DANIEL TRUEHART
Selden's Alabama Battery
Tarrant's Alabama Battery
Yates's Mississippi Battery

WADDELL'S BATTALION
MAJ. JAMES F. WADDELL
CAPT. OVERTON W. BARRETT
Bellamy's Alabama Battery
Emery's Alabama Battery
Barret's Missouri Battery

WHEELER'S CAVALRY CORPS
LT. COL. FELIX H. ROBERTSON
Huwald's Tennessee Battery
Ferrell's Georgia Battery
Tennessee Battery
Tennessee Battery
Wiggin's Arkansas Battery

JACKSON'S CAVALRY DIVISION
CAPT. JOHN WATIES
Croft's Georgia Battery
King's Missouri Battery
Watie's South Carolina Battery

GEORGIA STATE TROOPS
FIRST DIVISION GEORGIA MILITIA
MAJ. GEN. GUSTAVUS W. SMITH

FIRST BRIGADE
BRIG. GEN. REUBEN W. CARSWELL

SECOND BRIGADE
BRIG. GEN. PLEASANT J. PHILLIPS

THIRD BRIGADE
BRIG. GEN. CHARLES D. ANDERSON

FOURTH BRIGADE
BRIG. GEN. HENRY KENT McKAY

APPENDIX B

ORDER OF BATTLE FOR UNITED STATES FORCES DURING THE ATLANTA CAMPAIGN

MILITARY DIVISION OF THE MISSISSIPPI
MAJOR GENERAL WILLIAM T. SHERMAN

HEARQUARTERS GUARD
7TH COMPANY OHIO SHARPSHOOTERS, 1ST LT. WILLIAM MCCRORY

ARTILLERY
BRIG. GEN. WILLIAM F. BARRY, CHIEF OF ARTILLERY

ARMY OF THE CUMBERLAND
Maj. Gen. George H. Thomas

ESCORT
COMPANY I, 1ST OHIO CAVALRY, 1ST LT. HENRY C. REPPERT

ARTILLERY
BRIG. GEN. JOHN M. BRANNAN, CHIEF OF ARTILLERY

FOURTH ARMY CORPS
Maj. Gen. Oliver O. Howard
Maj. Gen. David S. Stanley (from 27 July)

FIRST DIVISION
MAJ. GEN. DAVID S. STANLEY
BRIG. GEN. WILLIAM GROSE
BRIG. GEN. NATHAN KIMBALL (FROM 4 AUGUST)

FIRST BRIGADE
BRIG. GEN. CHARLES CRUFT
COL. ISAAC M. KIRBY (FROM 10 JUNE)

21st Illinois
38th Illinois
31st Indiana
81st Indiana
1st Kentucky
2d Kentucky
90th Ohio
101st Ohio

SECOND BRIGADE
BRIG. GEN. WALTER C. WHITAKER
COL. JACOB TAYLOR (FROM 10 JUNE)

59th Illinois (to Third Brigade)
96th Illinois
115th Illinois
35th Indiana
84th Indiana
21st Kentucky
23d Kentucky
40th Ohio
45th Ohio
51st Ohio
99th Ohio

THIRD BRIGADE
BRIG. GEN. WILLIAM GROSE
COL. SIDNEY POST

59th Illinois (to Third Division)
75th Illinois
80th Illinois
84th Illinois
9th Indiana
30th Indiana
36th Indiana
84th Indiana
77th Pennsylvania

SECOND DIVISION
BRIG. GEN. JOHN NEWTON

¹ Of Polk's corps.

FIRST BRIGADE

COL. FRANCIS T. SHERMAN

BRIG. GEN. NATHAN KIMBALL (FROM 22 MAY)

COL. EMERSON OPDYKE (FROM 5 AUGUST)

36th Illinois

44th Illinois

73d Illinois

74th Illinois

88th Illinois

28th Kentucky (to Second Brigade)

2d Missouri

15th Missouri

24th Wisconsin

SECOND BRIGADE

BRIG. GEN. GEORGE D. WAGNER

COL. JOHN W. BLAKE (10–24 JULY)

100th Illinois

40th Indiana

57th Indiana

28th Kentucky

26th Ohio

97th Ohio

THIRD BRIGADE

BRIG. GEN. CHARLES C. HARKER (KILLED 27 JUNE)

COL. LUTHER BRADLEY

22d Illinois (mustered out 10 June)

27th Illinois (mustered out 27 August)

42d Illinois

51st Illinois

79th Illinois

3d Kentucky

64th Ohio

65th Ohio

125th Ohio

THIRD DIVISION

BRIG. GEN. THOMAS J. WOOD

FIRST BRIGADE

BRIG. GEN. AUGUST WILLICH (WOUNDED 15 MAY)

COL. WILLIAM H. GIBSON

COL. RICHARD H. NODINE

COL. CHARLES T. HOTCHKISS (FROM 25 AUGUST)

25th Illinois

35th Illinois

89th Illinois

32d Indiana

8th Kansas

15th Ohio

49th Ohio

15th Wisconsin

SECOND BRIGADE

BRIG. GEN. WILLIAM B. HAZEN (TRANSFERRED TO
THE ARMY OF THE TENNESSEE 17 AUGUST)

COL. SIDNEY POST

59th Indiana (from First Division)

6th Indiana

5th Kentucky

6th Kentucky

23d Kentucky

1st Ohio

6th Ohio

41st Ohio

71st Ohio

93d Ohio

124th Ohio

THIRD BRIGADE

BRIG. GEN. SAMUEL BEATTY

COL. FREDERICK KNEFLER (FROM 23 MAY)

79th Indiana

86th Indiana

9th Kentucky

17th Kentucky

13th Ohio

19th Ohio

59th Ohio

ARTILLERY BRIGADE (formed 26 July)
MAJ. THOMAS W. OSBORN
CAPT. LYMAN BRIDGES (FROM 30 JULY)
1st Illinois Light, Battery M
Illinois Light, Bridges Battery
Indiana Light, 5th Battery
1st Ohio Light, Battery A
1st Ohio Light, Battery M
Ohio Light, 6th Battery
Pennsylvania Light, Battery B

FOURTEENTH ARMY CORPS
MAJ. GEN. JOHN M. PALMER (RESIGNED 6 AUGUST)
BRIG. GEN. RICHARD W. JOHNSON
BREVET MAJ. GEN. JEFFERSON C. DAVIS (FROM 22 AUGUST)

FIRST DIVISION
BRIG. GEN. RICHARD W. JOHNSON
BRIG. GEN. JOHN H. KING
BRIG. GEN. WILLIAM P. CARLIN (FROM 17 AUGUST)

PROVOST GUARD
16TH U.S., CO. D, 1ST BATTALION, CAPT. CHARLES F. TROWBRIDGE

FIRST BRIGADE
BRIG. GEN. WILLIAM P. CARLIN
COL. ANSON G. MCCOOK (2–27 JULY)
COL. MARION C. TAYLOR (27 JULY–2 AUGUST)
104th Illinois
42d Indiana
88th Indiana
15th Kentucky
2d Ohio
33d Ohio
94th Ohio
10th Wisconsin
21st Wisconsin

SECOND BRIGADE

Brig. Gen. John H. King

Col. William L. Stoughton (wounded 4 July)

Col. Marshall F. Moore

Maj. John R. Edie

11th Michigan

69th Ohio

15th U.S. 1st and 3d Battalions

15th U.S. 2d Battalion

16th U.S. 1st Battalion

16th U.S. 2d Battalion

18th U.S. 1st and 3d Battalions

18th U.S. 2d Battalion

19th U.S. 1st Battalion and Co. A 2d Battalion

THIRD BRIGADE

Col. Benjamin F. Scribner

Col. Josiah Given (from 5 July)

Col. Marshall F. Moore (from 15 July)

37th Indiana

38th Indiana

21st Ohio

74th Ohio

78th Pennsylvania

79th Pennsylvania

1st Wisconsin

SECOND DIVISION

Brig. Gen. Jefferson C. Davis

Brig. Gen. James D. Morgan (from 22 August)

FIRST BRIGADE

Brig. Gen James D. Morgan

Col. Robert F. Smith

Col. Charles F. Lum (from 22 August)

10th Illinois (to Sixteenth Corps)

16th Illinois

60th Illinois

10th Michigan

14th Michigan

17th New York

SECOND BRIGADE
Col. John G. Mitchell
34th Illinois
78th Illinois
98th Ohio
108th Ohio
113th Ohio
121st Ohio

THIRD BRIGADE
Col. Daniel McCook (mortally wounded 27 June)
Col. Oscar F. Harmon (mortally wounded 27 June)
Col. Caleb J. Dilworth (wounded 1 September)
Lt. Col. James W. Langley
85th Illinois
86th Illinois
110th Illinois
125th Illinois
22d Indiana
52d Ohio

THIRD DIVISION
Brig. Gen. Absalom Baird

FIRST BRIGADE
Brig. Gen. John B. Turchin
Col. Moses B. Walker (from 15 July)
19th Illinois (mustered out 9 June)
24th Illinois (mustered out 28 June)
82d Indiana
23d Missouri
11th Ohio (mustered out 10 June)
17th Ohio
31st Ohio
89th Ohio
92d Ohio

SECOND BRIGADE

Col. Ferdinand Van Derveer

Col. Newell Gleason (from 27 June)

75th Indiana

87th Indiana

101st Indiana

2d Minnesota

9th Ohio (mustered out 22 May)

35th Ohio (mustered out 3 August)

105th Ohio

THIRD BRIGADE

Col. George P. Este

10th Indiana

74th Indiana

10th Kentucky

18th Kentucky

14th Ohio

38th Ohio

ARTILLERY BRIGADE (formed 24 July)

Maj. Charles Houghtalig

1st Illinois Light, Battery C

2d Illinois Light, Battery I

Indiana Light, 7th Battery

Indiana Light, 19th Battery

Indiana Light, 20th Battery

1st Ohio Light, Battery I

Wisconsin Light, 5th Battery

TWENTIETH ARMY CORPS

Maj. Gen. Joseph Hooker (resigned 27 July)

Brig. Gen. Alpheus S. Williams (from 28 July–27 August)

Maj. Gen. Henry W. Slocum

ESCORT

15th Illinois Cavalry, Company K, Capt. William Duncan

FIRST DIVISION
BRIG. GEN. ALPHEUS S. WILLIAMS
BRIG. GEN. JOSEPH F. KNIPE (28 JULY–27 AUGUST)

FIRST BRIGADE
BRIG. GEN. JOSEPH F. KNIPE
COL. WARREN PACKER (28 JULY–27 AUGUST)
5th Connecticut
3d Maryland (detachment)
123d New York
141st New York
46th Pennsylvania

SECOND BRIGADE
BRIG. GEN. THOMAS H. RUGER
27th Indiana
2d Massachusetts
13th New Jersey
107th New York
150th New York
3d Wisconsin

THIRD BRIGADE
COL. JAMES S. ROBINSON
COL. HORACE BOUGHTON
82d Illinois
101st Illinois
45th New York (at Nashville from 6 July)
143d New York
61st Ohio
82d Ohio
31st Wisconsin

SECOND DIVISION
BRIG. GEN. JOHN W. GEARY

FIRST BRIGADE
COL. CHARLES CANDY
COL. ARIO PARDEE, JR. (FROM 4 AUGUST)
5th Ohio

7th Ohio (mustered out 11 June)
29th Ohio
66th Ohio
28th Pennsylvania
147th Pennsylvania

SECOND BRIGADE
COL. ADOLPHUS BUSCHBECK
COL. JOHN T. LOCKMAN (FROM 22 MAY)
COL. PATRICK H. JONES (FROM 7 JUNE)
COL. GEORGE W. MINDIL (FROM 8 AUGUST)
33d New York
119th New York
134th New York
154th New York
27th Pennsylvania (mustered out 23 May)
73d Pennsylvania
109th Pennsylvania

THIRD BRIGADE
COL. DAVID IRELAND (WOUNDED 15 MAY)
COL. WILLIAM RICKARDS, JR.
COL. GEORGE A. COBHAM, JR. (16 MAY–5 JUNE)
60th New York
78th New York (consolidated with
the 102d New York 12 July)
102d New York
137th New York
149th New York
29th Pennsylvania
111th Pennsylvania

THIRD DIVISION
MAJ. GEN. DANIEL BUTTERFIELD
BRIG. GEN. WILLIAM T. WARD (FROM 29 JUNE)

FIRST BRIGADE
BRIG. GEN. WILLIAM T. WARD
COL. BENJAMIN HARRISON (FROM 29 JUNE)
102d Illinois

105th Illinois
129th Illinois
70th Indiana
79th Ohio

SECOND BRIGADE
COL. SAMUEL ROSS
COL. JOHN COBURN (FROM 9 MAY)
33d Indiana
85th Indiana
19th Michigan
22d Wisconsin

THIRD BRIGADE
COL. JAMES WOOD, JR.
20th Connecticut
33d Massachusetts
136th New York
55th Ohio
73d Ohio
26th Wisconsin

ARTILLERY BRIGADE (formed 27 July)
MAJ. JOHN A. REYNOLDS
1st Michigan Light, Battery I
1st New York Light, Battery I
1st New York Light, Battery M
New York Light, 13th Battery
1st Ohio Light, Battery C
Pennsylvania Light, Battery E
5th U.S. Battery K

UNATTACHED TROOPS

RESERVE BRIGADE
COL. JOSEPH W. BURKE
COL. HEBER LE FAVOUR (FROM 31 MAY)
10th Ohio (mustered out 27 May)
9th Michigan
22d Michigan

PONTONIERS

COL. GEORGE P. BUELL

58TH INDIANA

PONTOON BATTALION

SIEGE ARTILLERY

11TH INDIANA BATTERY, CAPT. ARNOLD SUTERMEISTER

AMMUNITION TRAIN GUARD

1ST BATTALION OHIO SHARPSHOOTERS, CAPT. GERSHOM M. BARBER

CAVALRY CORPS

BRIG. GEN. WASHINGTON L. ELLIOTT

ESCORT

4TH OHIO CAVALRY, COMPANY D, CAPT. PHILIP H. WARNER

FIRST DIVISION
BRIG. GEN. EDWARD M. McCOOK

FIRST BRIGADE

COL. JOSEPH B. DORR (CAPTURED 30 JULY)

LT. COL. JAMES P. BROWNLOW (FROM 30 JULY–12 AUGUST)

BRIG. GEN. JOHN T. CROXTON

8th Iowa

4th Kentucky Mounted Infantry (from 30 June)

2d Michigan (at Franklin, TN from 29 June)

1st Tennessee

SECOND BRIGADE

COL. OSCAR H. LA GRANGE (CAPTURED 6 MAY)

LT. COL. JAMES W. STEWART (CAPTURED 26 MAY)

LT. COL. HORACE P. LAMSON

LT. COL. WILLIAM H. TORREY (21–30 JULY)

2d Indiana

4th Indiana

1st Wisconsin

THIRD BRIGADE
COL. LOUIS D. WATKINS
COL. JOHN K. FAULKNER (5 JULY–10 AUGUST)
4th Kentucky
6th Kentucky
7th Kentucky

ARTILLERY
18TH INDIANA BATTERY, LT. WILLIAM B. RIPPETOE

SECOND DIVISION
BRIG. GEN. KENNER GARRARD

FIRST BRIGADE
COL. ROBERT H. G. MINTY
4th Michigan
7th Pennsylvania
4th U.S.

SECOND BRIGADE
COL. ELI LONG (WOUNDED 20 AUGUST)
COL. BEROTH B. EGGLESTON
1st Ohio
3d Ohio
4th Ohio

THIRD BRIGADE (mounted infantry)
COL. JOHN T. WILDER
COL. ABRAM O. MILLER (FROM 14 JUNE)
98th Illinois
123d Illinois
17th Indiana
72d Indiana

ARTILLERY
CHICAGO BOARD OF TRADE BATTERY, LT. GEORGE I. ROBINSON

THIRD DIVISION
BRIG. GEN. JUDSON KILPATRICK (WOUNDED 13 MAY)
COL. ELI H. MURRAY (13–21 MAY)
COL. WILLIAM W. LOWE (FROM 21 MAY–23 JULY)

FIRST BRIGADE
LT. COL. ROBERT KLIEN
LT. COL. MATTHEWSON T. PATRICK
MAJ. J. MORRIS YOUNG
3d Indiana (four companies)
5th Iowa

SECOND BRIGADE
COL. CHARLES C. SMITH
MAJ. THOMAS H. SANDERSON (2 JULY–6 AUGUST)
LT. COL. FIELDER A. JONES
8th Indiana
2d Kentucky
10th Ohio

THIRD BRIGADE
COL. ELI H. MURRAY
COL. SMITH D. ATKINS (13–21 MAY)
92d Illinois (mounted infantry)
3d Kentucky
5th Kentucky

ARTILLERY
10TH WISCONSIN BATTERY, CAPT. YATES V. BEEBE

ARMY OF THE TENNESSEE
MAJ. GEN. JAMES B. MCPHERSON (KILLED 22 JULY)
MAJ. GEN. JOHN A. LOGAN (22–27 JULY)
MAJ. GEN. OLIVER O. HOWARD (FROM 27 JULY)

ESCORT
4TH CO. OHIO CAVALRY, CAPT. JOHN S. FOSTER, CAPT. JOHN L. KING
1ST OHIO CAVALRY, CO. B, CAPT. GEORGE F. CONN

FIFTEENTH ARMY CORPS
Maj. Gen. John A. Logan
Brig. Gen. Morgan L. Smith (22–27 July)

FIRST DIVISION
Maj. Gen. Peter J. Osterhaus
Brig. Gen. Charles R. Woods (15 July–15 August)

FIRST BRIGADE
Brig. Gen. Charles R. Woods
(assigned to Sixteenth Corps 22 August)
Col. Milo Smith (15 July–15 August; from 22 August)
26th Iowa
30th Iowa
27th Missouri
6th Ohio

SECOND BRIGADE
Col. James A. Williamson
4th Iowa
9th Iowa
25th Iowa
31st Iowa

THIRD BRIGADE
Col. Hugo Wangelin
3d Missouri
12th Missouri
17th Missouri
29th Missouri
31st Missouri
32d Missouri

ARTILLERY
Maj. Clemens Landgraeber
2d Missouri Light, Battery F
Ohio Light, 4th Battery

SECOND DIVISION
BRIG. GEN. MORGAN L. SMITH
BRIG. GEN. JOSEPH A. J. LIGHTBURN (22–27 JULY)
BRIG. GEN. WILLIAM B. HAZEN (FROM 17 AUGUST)

FIRST BRIGADE
BRIG. GEN. GILES A. SMITH
(TO FOURTH DIVISION, SEVENTEENTH CORPS 20 JULY)
COL. JAMES S. MARTIN
COL. THEODORE JONES (FROM 4 AUGUST)
55th Illinois
111th Illinois (to Second Brigade 4 August)
116th Illinois
127th Illinois
6th Missouri
8th Missouri
30th Ohio
57th Ohio

SECOND BRIGADE
BRIG. GEN. JOSEPH A. J. LIGHTBURN (WOUNDED 4 AUGUST)
COL. WELLS JONES (22–27 JULY, FROM 4 AUGUST)
111th Illinois
83d Indiana
30th Ohio (to First Brigade 4 August)
37th Ohio
47th Ohio
53d Ohio
54th Ohio

ARTILLERY
CAPT. FRANCIS DE GRESS
1st Illinois Light, Battery A
1st Illinois Light, Battery B
1st Illinois Light, Battery H

THIRD DIVISION
(SERVED IN REAR AREAS THROUGHOUT THE CAMPAIGN)
BRIG. GEN. JOHN E. SMITH

ESCORT

4TH MISSOURI, CO. F, LT. ALEXANDER MUELLER

FIRST BRIGADE

COL. JESSE I. ALEXANDER

COL. JOSEPH B. McCOWN (FROM 1 SEPTEMBER)

63d Illinois

48th Indiana

59th Indiana

4th Minnesota

18th Wisconsin

SECOND BRIGADE

COL. GREEN B. RAUM

13th Illinois (detachment)

56th Illinois

17th Iowa

10th Missouri

24th Missouri, Co. E

80th Ohio

THIRD BRIGADE

BRIG. GEN. CHARLES L. MATTHIES

COL. BENJAMIN D. DEAN (15–31 MAY, FROM 25 JULY)

COL. JABEZ BANBURY (1 JUNE–25 JULY)

93d Illinois

5th Iowa (transferred 12 July)

10th Iowa

26th Missouri

ARTILLERY

CAPT. HENRY DILLON

Wisconsin Light, 6th Battery

Wisconsin Light, 12th Battery

CAVALRY

5TH OHIO, COL. THOMAS T. HEATH

FOURTH DIVISION
Brig. Gen. William Harrow

FIRST BRIGADE
Col. Reuben Williams
Col. John M. Oliver (from 4 August)
26th Illinois (to Second Brigade 4 August)
90th Illinois
12th Indiana
100th Indiana (to Second Brigade 4 August)

SECOND BRIGADE
Brig. Gen. Charles C. Walcutt
40th Illinois
103d Illinois
97th Indiana
6th Iowa
46th Ohio

THIRD BRIGADE
(merged with First Brigade 4 August)
Col. John M. Oliver
48th Illinois
99th Indiana
15th Michigan
70th Ohio

ARTILLERY
Capt. Henry H. Griffiths
Capt. Josiah H. Burton (from 11 August)
1st Illinois Light, Battery F
Iowa Light, 1st Battery

SIXTEENTH ARMY CORPS
Maj. Gen. Grenville Dodge (wounded 19 August)
Brig. Gen. Thomas E. G. Ransom

GENERAL HEADQUARTERS
1ST ALABAMA CAVALRY, LT. COL. GEORGE L. GODFREY,
COL. GEORGE E. SPENCER
52D ILLINOIS, CO. A, CAPT. GEORGE E. YOUNG

SECOND DIVISION
BRIG. GEN. THOMAS W. SWEENEY
BRIG. GEN. ELLIOTT W. RICE (25 JULY)
BRIG. GEN. JOHN M. CORSE (FROM 26 JULY)

FIRST BRIGADE
BRIG. GEN. ELLIOTT W. RICE

52d Illinois

66th Indiana

2d Iowa

7th Iowa

SECOND BRIGADE
COL. PATRICK E. BURKE (MORTALLY WOUNDED 16 MAY)

LT. COL. ROBERT N. ADAMS

COL. AUGUST MERSY (23 MAY–24 JULY)

9th Illinois (mounted)

12th Illinois

66th Illinois

81st Ohio

THIRD BRIGADE
COL. MOSES M. BANE

BRIG. GEN. WILLIAM VANDEVER (20 JUNE–2 AUGUST)

COL. HENRY J. B. CUMMINGS (3–15 AUGUST)

COL. RICHARD ROWETT (FROM 15 AUGUST)

7th Illinois

50th Illinois

57th Illinois

39th Iowa

ARTILLERY

CAPT. FREDERICK WELKER

1st Michigan Light, Battery B

1st Missouri Light, Battery H

1st Missouri Light, Battery I

FOURTH DIVISION

BRIG. GEN. JAMES C. VEATCH (SICK FROM 17 JULY)

BRIG. GEN. JOHN W. FULLER

BRIG. GEN. THOMAS E. G. RANSOM (4–20 AUGUST)

FIRST BRIGADE

BRIG. GEN. JOHN W. FULLER

COL. JOHN MORRILL (WOUNDED 22 JULY)

LT. COL. HENRY T. McDOWELL

64th Illinois

18th Missouri

27th Ohio

39th Ohio

SECOND BRIGADE

BRIG. GEN. JOHN W. SPRAGUE

35th New Jersey

43d Ohio

63d Ohio

25th Wisconsin

THIRD BRIGADE

COL. JAMES H. HOWE

COL. WILLIAM T. C. GROWER (21 JULY–19 AUGUST)

COL. JOHN TILLSON (FROM 20 AUGUST)

10th Illinois

25th Indiana

17th New York (to Fourteenth Corps 2 August)

32d Wisconsin

ARTILLERY

CAPT. JEROME B. BURROWS

CAPT. GEORGE ROBINSON (FROM 3 JULY)

1st Michigan Light, Battery C

Ohio Light, 14th Battery

2d U.S., Battery F

SEVENTEENTH ARMY CORPS
MAJ. GEN. FRANK P. BLAIR, JR.

ESCORT
1st Ohio Cavalry, Co. M, Lt. Charles H. Shultz

9th Illinois (mounted infantry), Co. G, Capt. Isaac Clements

11th Illinois Cavalry, Co. G, Capt. Stephen S. Tripp

THIRD DIVISION
Brig. Gen. Mortimer Leggett
Brig. Gen. Charles R. Woods (from 23 August)

ESCORT
1st Ohio Cavalry, Co. D, Lt. James W. Kirkendall

FIRST BRIGADE
Brig. Gen. Manning F. Force (wounded 22 July)

Col. George E. Bryant

20th Illinois

30th Illinois

31st Illinois

45th Illinois

12th Wisconsin

16th Wisconsin

SECOND BRIGADE
Col. Robert K. Scott (captured 22 July)

Lt. Col. Greenberry F. Wiles

20th Ohio

32d Ohio (to Fourth Division 10 July)

68th Ohio

78th Ohio

THIRD BRIGADE
Col. Adam G. Malloy

17th Wisconsin

Worden's Battalion

ARTILLERY
CAPT. WILLIAM S. WILLIAMS
1st Illinois Light, Battery D
1st Michigan Light, Battery H
Ohio Light, 3d Battery

FOURTH DIVISION
BRIG. GEN. WALTER Q. GRESHAM (WOUNDED 20 JULY)
COL. WILLIAM HALL
BRIG. GEN. GILES A. SMITH (FROM 22 JULY)

ESCORT
11TH ILLINOIS CAVALRY, CO. G, CAPT. STEPHEN S. TRIPP

FIRST BRIGADE
COL. WILLIAM L. SANDERSON
COL. BENJAMIN F. POTTS (FROM 18 JULY)
32d Illinois (to Second Brigade 18 July)
53d Illinois
23d Indian
53d Indiana
3d Iowa
12th Wisconsin (to Third Division 10 July)

SECOND BRIGADE
COL. GEORGE C. ROGERS
COL. ISAAC C. PUGH (5–19 JULY)
COL. JOHN LOGAN
14th Illinois
15th Illinois
32d Illinois
41st Illinois
53d Illinois (to First Brigade 18 July)

THIRD BRIGADE
COL. WILLIAM HALL
COL. JOHN SHANE (21 JULY)
BRIG. GEN. WILLIAM W. BELKNAP (FROM 31 JULY)
11th Iowa
13th Iowa

15th Iowa
16th Iowa

ARTILLERY
CAPT. EDWARD SPEAR, JR.
CAPT. WILLIAM Z. CLAYTON (FROM 25 AUGUST)
2d Illinois Light, Battery F
Minnesota Light, 1st Battery
1st Missouri Light, Battery C
Ohio Light, 10th Battery
Ohio Light, 15th Battery

ARMY OF THE OHIO
MAJ. GEN. JOHN M. SCHOFIELD

ESCORT
7TH OHIO CAVALRY, COMPANY G, CAPT. JOHN A. ASHBURY

ENGINEER BATTALION
CAPT. CHARLES E. MCALESTER
CAPT. OLIVER S. MCCLURE (FROM 23 JUNE)

FIRST DIVISION
(OFFICIALLY DISBANDED 11 AUGUST, TROOPS DISTRIBUTED BETWEEN SECOND AND
THIRD DIVISIONS FROM 9 JUNE.
BRIG. GEN. ALVIN P. HOVEY (ON LEAVE FROM 9 JUNE)

FIRST BRIGADE
(WITH THIRD DIVISION FROM 9 JUNE)
COL. RICHARD F. BARTER
120th Indiana
124th Indiana
128th Indiana

SECOND BRIGADE
(WITH SECOND DIVISION FROM 9 JUNE)
COL. JOHN C. MCQUISTON
COL. PETER T. SWAINE (FROM 23 JUNE)

123d Indiana
129th Indiana
130th Indiana
99th Ohio

ARTILLERY
Indiana Light, 23d Battery
Indiana Light, 24th Battery

SECOND DIVISION
Brig. Gen. Henry M. Judah
Brig. Gen. Milo S. Hascall (from 18 May)

FIRST BRIGADE
Brig. Gen. Nathaniel C. McLean
Brig. Gen. Joseph A. Cooper (from 4 June)
80th Indiana (to Second Brigade 8 June)
91st Indiana (to Third Brigade 11 August)
13th Kentucky (to Second Brigade 8 June)
14th Kentucky
25th Michigan
45th Ohio (to Fourth Corps 22 June)
3d Tennessee
6th Tennessee

SECOND BRIGADE
Brig. Gen Milo S. Haskall
Col. John R. Bond (from 18 May)
Col. William E. Hobson (18 June–15 August)
107th Illinois
80th Indiana
13th Kentucky
23d Michigan
45th Ohio (to First Brigade 8 June)
111th Ohio
118th Ohio

THIRD BRIGADE
Col. Silas Strickland
91st Indiana

14th Kentucky (to First Brigade 11 August)
20th Kentucky
27th Kentucky
50th Ohio

ARTILLERY
Capt. Joseph C. Shields
Indiana Light, 22d Battery
1st Michigan Light, Battery F
Ohio Light, 19th Battery

THIRD DIVISION
Brig. Gen. Jacob D. Cox

FIRST BRIGADE
Col. James W. Reilly
112th Illinois (to Third Brigade 11 August)
11th Kentucky
12th Kentucky
16th Kentucky
100th Ohio
104th Ohio
8th Tennessee

SECOND BRIGADE
Brig. Gen. Mahlon D. Manson (wounded 14 May)
Col. John S. Hurt (14–16, 18–21 May)
Brig. Gen. Milo S. Hascall (17–18 May)
Col. John S. Casement (21 May–4 June, from 31 July)
Col. John Cameron (4 June–31 July)
12th Illinois
65th Illinois
63d Indiana (to Third Brigade 11 August)
65th Indiana
24th Kentucky
103d Ohio
5th Tennessee (to Third Brigade 5 June)

THIRD BRIGADE
BRIG. GEN. NATHANIEL C. MCLEAN (TRANSFERRED 17 JUNE)
COL. ROBERT K. BYRD
COL. ISRAEL N. STILES
12th Illinois
63d Indiana
11th Kentucky (to First Brigade 11 August)
12th Kentucky (to First Brigade 11 August)
1st Tennessee (mustered out 11 August)
5th Tennessee

ARTILLERY
MAJ. HENRY W. WELLS
Indiana Light, 15th Battery
1st Ohio Light, Battery D

CAVALRY DIVISION
MAJ. GEN. GEORGE STONEMAN (CAPTURED 31 JULY)
COL. HORACE CAPRON (1–11 AUGUST)
COL. ISRAEL GARRARD (FROM 11 AUGUST)

ESCORT
7TH OHIO, COMPANY D, LT. SAMUEL MURPHY, LT. W. W. MANNING

FIRST BRIGADE
COL. ISRAEL GARRARD
COL. GEORGE S, ACKER (FROM 11 AUGUST)
9th Michigan
7th Ohio

SECOND BRIGADE
COL. JAMES BIDDLE (CAPTURED 31 JULY)
16th Illinois
5th Indiana
6th Indiana
12th Kentucky

THIRD BRIGADE
COL. HORACE CAPRON
14th Illinois

8th Michigan

McLaughlin's Ohio Squdron

INDEPENDENT BRIGADE

COL. ALEXANDER W. HOLEMAN

LT. COL. SILAS ADAMS

1st Kentucky

11th Kentucky

ARTILLERY

CAPT. ALEXANDER HARDY (CAPTURED 31 JULY)

LT. HIRAM ALLEN

24th Indiana Battery

BIBLIOGRAPHY

Blanchard, Ira. *I Marched with Sherman: Civil War Memoirs of the 20th Illinois Volunteer Infantry*. San Francisco: J. D. Huff and Company, 1992.

Buck, Irving A., ed. *Cleburne and His Command*. Jackson, TN.: McCowat-Mercer Press, 1959.

Castel, Albert. *Decision in the West: The Atlanta Campaign of 1864*. Lawrence: University Press of Kansas, 1992.

Chesnut, Mary Boykin. *Mary Chesnut's Civil War*. Edited by C. Vann Woodward. New Haven, CT.: Yale University Press, 1981.

Connelly, Thomas L. *Army of the Heartland: The Army of Tennessee, 1861–1862*. Baton Rouge: Louisiana State University Press, 1967.

_____. *Autumn of Glory: The Army of Tennessee, 1862–1865*. Baton Rouge: Louisiana State University Press, 1971.

Connolly, James A. *Three Years in the Army of the Cumberland: The Letters and Diary of Major James A. Connolly*. Edited by Paul M. Angle. Bloomington: Indiana University Press, 1959.

Cox, Jacob D. *Sherman's Battle for Atlanta*. New York: Da Capo Press, 1994.

Cozzens, Peter. *The Terrible Sound: The Battle of Chickamauga*. Urbana: University of Illinois Press, 1992.

_____. *The Shipwreck of Their Hopes: The Battles for Chattanooga*. Urbana: University of Illinois Press, 1994.

Daniel, Larry J. *Soldiering in the Army of Tennessee*. Chapel Hill: University of North Carolina Press, 1991.

Davis, William C. *Jefferson Davis: The Man and His Hour*. New York: HarperCollins, 1991.

_____. ed. *The Confederate General*. 6 vols. National Historical Society, 1991.

Dyer, John P. *The Gallant Hood*. Indianapolis: Bobbs-Merrill, 1950.

Foote, Shelby. *The Civil War, A Narrative: Fort Sumter to Perryville*. New York: Random House, 1958.

_____. *The Civil War, A Narrative: Fredericksburg to Meridian*. New York: Random House, 1963.

_____. *The Civil War, A Narrative: Red River to Appomattox*. New York: Randon House, 1974.

Freeman, Douglas Southall. *R. E. Lee*. 4 vols. New York: Charles Scribner's Sons, 1935.

_____. *Lee's Lieutenants: A Study in Command*. 3 vols. New York: Charles Scribner's Sons, 1944.

Geary, John White. *A Politician Goes to War: The Civil War Letters of John White Geary*. Edited by William Alan Blair; selections and introduction by Bell Irvin Wiley. University Park: Pennsylvania State University Press, 1995.

Glatthaar, Joseph T. *The March to the Sea and Beyond: Sherman's Troops in the Savannah and Carolinas Campaigns*. New York: New York University Press, 1985.

Govan, Gilbert E., and James W. Livingood. *A Different Valor: The Story of Joseph E. Johnston, C.S.A.*. Indianapolis: Bobbs-Merrill, 1956.

Grant, Ulysses S. *Personal Memoirs of U. S. Grant*. 2 vols. New York: Charles A. Webster & Co., 1885.

Hallock, Judith Lee. *Braxton Bragg and Confederate Defeat, Volume II*. Tuscaloosa: University of Alabama Press, 1991.

Hattaway, Herman. *General Stephen D. Lee*. Jackson: University Press of Mississippi, 1983.

Hay, Thomas R. *Hood's Tennessee Campaign*. Dayton, OH.: Press of he Morningside Bookshop, 1976.

Hood, John Bell. *Advance and Retreat: Personal Experiences in the United States and Confederate States Armies*. Bloomington: Indiana University Press, 1959.

Horn, Stanley F. *The Army of Tennessee*. Indianapolis: Bobbs-Merrill Co., 1941.

_____. *The Decisive Battle of Nashville*. Baton Rouge: Louisiana State University Press, 1956.

Hughes, Nathaniel Cheairs, Jr. *General William J. Hardee, Old Reliable*. Baton Rouge: Louisiana State University Press, 1965.

Losson, Christopher. *Tennessee's Forgotten Warriors: Frank Cheatham and His Confederate Division.* Knoxville: University of Tennessee Press, 1989.

Johnston, Joseph E. *Narrative of Military Operations During the Civil War.* New York: Da Capo Press, 1990.

Jones, John B. *A Rebel War Clerk's Diary.* Edited by Earl Schenck Miers. Baton Rouge: Louisiana State University Press, 1993.

Keen, Robert Garlick Hill. *Inside the Confederate Government: The Diary of Robert Garlick Hill Keen.* Edited by Edward Younger. Baton Rouge: Louisiana State University Press, 1993.

Manigault, Arthur Middleton. *A Carolinian Goes to War: The Civil War Narrative of Arthur Middleton Manigault.* Edited by R. Lockwood Tower; Forward by Thomas L.Connelly. Columbia: University of South Carolina Press,1983.

McMurry, Richard M. *John Bell Hood and the War for Southern Independence.* Lexington: University of Kentucky Press, 1982.

_____. *Two Great Rebel Armies: An Essay in Confederate Military History.* Chapel Hill: University of North Carolina Press, 1989.

McWhiney, Grady. *Braxton Bragg and Confederate Defeat.* New York: Columbia University Press, 1969.

_____, and Perry D. Jamieson. *Attack and Die: Civil War Military Tactics and the Southern Heritage.* Tuscaloosa: University of Alabama Press, 1982.

Marszalek, John F. *Sherman: A Soldier's Passion for Order.* New York: The Free Press, 1993.

Pfanz, Harry L. *Gettysburg, The Second Day.* Chapel Hill: University of North Carolina Press, 1987.

Scaife, William R. *The Campaign for Atlanta.* Saline, MI.: McNaughton & Gunn, Inc., 1993.

Sherman, William T. *Memoirs of General William T. Sherman.* 2 vols. Bloomington: Indiana University Press, 1957.

Simpson, Harold B. *Cry Comanche: the 2nd U.S. Cavalry in Texas, 1855–1861.* Hillsboro, TX.: Hill College Press, 1988.

Sword, Wiley. *Embrace an Angry Wind: The Confederacy's Last Hurrah: Spring Hill, Franklin, and Nashville.* New York: HarperCollins, 1992.

Symonds, Craig L. *Joseph E. Johnston: A Civil War Biography.* New York: W. W. Norton, 1992.

Strayer, Larry M. and Richard A. Baumgartner. *Echoes of Battle: The Atlanta Campaign.* Huntington, WV: Blue Acorn Press, 1991.

Watkins, Sam R. *"Co. Aytch": A Sideshow of the Big Show.* New York: Collier Books, 1962.

Woodworth, Steven E. *Jefferson Davis and His Generals: The Failure of Confederate Command in the West.* Lawrence: University Press of Kansas, 1991.

_____. *A Deep Steady Thunder: The Battle of Chickamauga.* Fort Worth: Ryan Place Publishers, Inc., 1996.

PHOTO CREDITS

We gratefully acknowledge the cooperation of the United States Army Military History Institute at Carlisle Barracks, Pennsylvania, and the assistance of Jim Enos for photographs of Francis P. Blair, Benjamin Franklin Cheatham, Jacob D. Cox, Jefferson Davis, Jefferson C. Davis, William J. Hardee, John Bell Hood, Joseph Hooker, Oliver O. Howard, Alfred Iverson, Joseph E. Johnston, Judson Kilpatrick, Stephen D. Lee, John A. Logan, James B. McPherson, Leonidas Polk, John M. Schofield, A.P. Stewart, George Stoneman, and Joseph Wheeler.

We credit the Library of Congress for photographs of Braxton Bragg, Patrick Cleburne, Arthur Manigault, William T. Sherman, and George H. Thomas.

INDEX

Acworth, Ga., 45

Adairsville, Ga., 43

Advance and Retreat, 113

Alabama, 27, 63, 111, 114

Allatoona Pass, 43, 45

Anderson, Patton, 88, 91, 105

Andersonville Prison, 51, 94

Antietam, Battle of, 17, 114

Arkansas, U.S. Department of the, 24

Armies, C.S.:

    Army of Mississippi, 37, 42, 88

    Army of Northern Virginia, 23, 28, 49

    Army of Tennessee, 13, 20, 23, 26–27, 30–31, 37, 42, 49–50,
        55–56, 61, 63, 86, 88, 115

Armies, U.S.:

    Army of the Cumberland (Thomas's), 33, 35, 61–62, 64, 71,
        85, 102, 106–107, 111

    Army of the Ohio (Schofield's), 34, 43, 62, 98, 111

    Army of the Tennessee (McPherson's, Howard's), 33, 37, 62,
        71, 73, 77, 85, 89, 93, 104, 109

Armies of the United States (U.S. Army), 16, 23, 25–26, 115

Atlanta, Battle of, 75–86, 87, 114

Atlanta, Ga., 33, 46–48, 51, 54–55, 57, 59, 61–64, 70–75, 85, 87,
    89–91, 94, 96–100, 102–103, 106–107, 109, 110–115

Atlanta Campaign, 112, 115

Atlanta & West Point Railroad, 62, 94, 103

Augusta, Ga., 62

Bald Hill, 74, 79

Bate, William, 69, 99

Beauregard, P.G.T., 48, 113

Big Round Top, 18

Blair, Francis P. (Frank), 77, 85, 114

Bragg, Braxton, 13, 18, 20, 23, 26–27, 30, 49–52, 54–55

Breckinridge, John C., 16

Brigades, C.S.:
   Featherston's (Mississippi), 69
   Ferguson's (cavalry), 109
   Gibson's (Louisiana), 92
   Govan's (Arkansas), 79, 107, 109
   Granbury's (Texas), 107
   Hood's (Texas), 17
   Lewis's (Kentucky, "Orphan Brigade"), 107, 109
   Maney's (Tennessee), 79
   Manigault's, 80, 92
   O'Neal's, 70
   Reynolds's (Arkansas), 70
   Ross's (Texas, cavalry), 99, 102
   Sharp's (Mississippi), 80
   Stevens's (Georgia), 69
   Scott's, 69
   Vaughn's (Tennessee), 79
Brigades, U.S. (see Appendix B for numeric designations):
   Ireland's, 69
   Jones's, 80
   Lightburn's, 91
   Martin's, 80, 91
   Reilly's, 98
   Walcutt's, 77
Brown, John C., 80–81, 83–84, 88, 91, 105

California, 15
Calhoun, Ga., 42, 43
Carolinas, the, 114–115
Cassville, Ga., 43, 52
Cavalry, C.S., 16, 27, 37–38, 42, 61,65, 73–74, 94, 96, 99–100, 102
Cavalry, U.S., 16, 34, 43, 89–90, 94, 96, 100, 102
Chancellorsville, Battle of, 17, 74, 86
Chattahoochee River, 46, 48, 51, 103
Chattanooga, Tn., 23, 26, 33–34, 62, 100, 111
Cheatham, Benjamin F. (Frank), 61, 64, 67, 74, 79, 80, 87, 93

Chesnut, Mary Boykin, 17, 18, 20
Chickamauga, Battle of, 13, 18, 20–21, 23, 71, 114
Clayton, Henry, 80, 82, 83–84, 92–93
Cleburne, Patrick, 45, 77, 104, 105, 109
Comanches, 16
Commissary Department, Army of Tennessee, 63
Congress, C.S., 26, 55
Congress, U.S., 14
Connolly, James A., 47
Cooper, Samuel, 55
Corps, C.S.:
    Cheatham's, 74, 82, 84, 114
    Hardee's, 37, 45, 61, 64–65, 74–75, 84, 88, 99, 103, 104,
        107–109
    Hood's, 37, 42, 61, 79, 87
    Longstreet's, 18
    Lee's, 90, 99, 103–104, 107, 110
    Polk's (see Armies, C.S.: Army of Mississippi)
    Stewart's, 64, 67, 69, 74, 88, 90, 93, 109, 110
Corps, U.S.:
    Fourth (Howard's, Stanley's), 45, 67, 89, 103, 106, 108–109
    Fourteenth (Palmer's, Davis's), 67, 98, 107–108
    Fifteenth (Logan's), 77, 79, 80, 82, 91, 93, 105
    Sixteenth (Dodge's), 75, 83, 93
    Seventeenth (Blair's), 77, 93
    Twentieth (Hooker's, Slocum's), 45, 67, 70, 103, 110
    Twenty-third (Schofield's), 35, 37, 67, 106
Cox, Jacob D., 39, 46, 98–99, 103, 106, 112
Cumberland, U.S. Department of the, 23

Dallas, Ga., 45
Dalton, Ga., 20, 29, 33, 35, 37, 39, 42, 61, 100, 111
Davis, Jefferson, 20, 26–30, 37, 48–55, 57, 88, 100, 113, 115
Davis, Jefferson C., 108–109
Decatur, Ga., 62, 65, 74–75, 84, 94, 96, 102
Decatur Road, 67, 74
Degress, Francis, 80, 83–84

Degress's Illinois Battery, 80
Department of War, C.S., 57
Divisions, C.S.:
    Bate's, 69, 77, 99
    Brown's, 80
    Cheatham's, 69, 88
    Clayton's, 80, 92
    Cleburne's, 45, 69–70, 73–75, 77, 84
    French's, 109
    Hood's, 18
    Hindman's, 88, 91, 105
    Jackson's (cavalry), 42, 100
    Loring's, 69, 93
    Maney's, 69, 74–75, 77, 84
    Stevenson's, 80
    Stewart's, 80
    Walthall's, 70, 93
    Walker's, 69, 70, 75, 77, 88
Divisions, U.S. (see Appendix B for numeric designations):
    2d, Fifteenth Corps (Morgan Smith's), 80, 91
    Cox's, 98, 106
    Garrard's (cavalry), 89, 102
    Geary's, 67, 69
    Hascall's, 98–99, 106
    Kilpatrick's (cavalry), 102
    Leggett's, 77, 79
    Newton's, 67, 71
    McCook's (cavalry), 89, 96
    Smith's (Giles Smith), 77, 79
    Stoneman's (cavalry), 89, 96
    Ward's, 67, 69
    Williams's, 67
Dodge, Grenville, 75, 77

East Point, Ga., 90, 93, 98–99
East Tennessee & Georgia Railroad, 35
Etowah River, 43
Ezra Church (and Battle of), 91, 93–94

Featherston, Winfield Scott, 66, 69, 72
Ferguson, Samuel, 109
Flat Rock, Ga., 94
Flint River, 103
Florida, 88
Fort Jones, Ca., 15
Fort Sumter, SC., 90
Franklin, Battle of, 111
Fredericksburg, Battle of, 17
French, Samuel, 109
Fuller, John, 75, 77

Gaines' Mill, Battle of, 17
Garrard, Kenner, 16, 89, 94, 102
Geary, John, 67, 69, 70
Georgia, 13, 18, 20, 26–27, 30–31, 55, 111, 113, 115
Georgia Militia, 54, 61, 65, 74, 80
Georgia Railroad, 62, 64, 80
Gettysburg, Battle of, 17–18, 23, 114
Gibson, Randall, 92, 105
Govan, Daniel, 79, 107, 109
Granbury, Hiram, 107
Grant, Ulysses S., 23–25, 56, 61, 97, 111, 115

Halleck, Henry, 99, 110
Hardee, William J., 16, 26–27, 30, 37, 42–43, 49–52, 54–55, 61,
    64–65, 67, 69, 70–71, 74–75, 79–80, 85, 88, 93, 103–110,
    114–115
Hascall, Milo, 98–99, 106
Hell Hole, the (see New Hope Church)
Hill, D.H., 20
Hindman, Thomas C., 27–29, 80
Hood, Anna Marie Hennen, 116
Hood, John Bell, 13–18, 20–21, 29–31, 33–34, 37, 42–43, 45–46,
    49–50, 52–57, 59, 61–65, 67, 69–75, 77, 79–80, 84–89,
    90–91, 93–94, 96–100, 102–103, 106–107, 109–116
Hood, Lydia, 116

Hooker, Joseph, 67, 89
Howard, O.O., 67, 89–91, 93, 103–104, 106–107, 109

Ireland, David, 69
Iverson, Alfred, 94, 96, 99

Jackson, Thomas J. (Stonewall), 13, 73, 85, 113
Jackson, William H. (Red), 42, 96, 100, 102
Jefferson Barracks, Mo., 16
Johnston, Albert Sidney, 16
Johnston, Joseph E., 23–24, 26–31, 33, 35, 37–39, 42–43,
    45–57, 59, 61, 86–87, 106, 112–115
Jones, John B., 13, 14, 22
Jones, Wells, 80
Jonesboro, Ga. (and Battle of), 102, 103, 105–109

Kennesaw Mountain, Ga. (and Battle of), 46
Kentucky, 16, 30
Kilpatrick, Hugh Judson, 102
Kolb's Farm, Battle of, 46

Lee, Fitzhugh, 16
Lee, Robert E., 15–18, 20, 23, 26, 28, 33, 49, 56, 59, 65,
    71, 85, 97, 113, 114
Lee, Stephen D., 87, 90–93, 105, 107, 114
Leggett, Mortimer, 77
Lewis, Joseph, 107
Lick Skillet Road, 91
Lightburn, Joseph, 80
Lincoln, Abraham, 23, 97, 111
Little Round Top, 18
Logan, John A. (Black Jack), 77, 82–83, 88–89, 93, 105
Longstreet, James, 18, 20
Loring, W.W., 69, 93
Louisiana, 116
Louisville, Ky., 34
Lovejoy's Station, 94, 96, 102, 109–110

Mackall, W.W., 87

Macon, Ga., 59, 94, 96, 107

Macon & Western Railroad, 62, 89, 98, 103, 106–107, 109

Manassas, First Battle of (Bull Run), 26

Manassas, Second Battle of (Bull Run), 17, 86

Maney, George, 69, 79

Manigault, Arthur, 80–84, 105–106

Marietta, Ga., 100

Martin, James, 80

McCook, Edward, 89, 94, 96, 102

McDonough Road, 107

McPherson, James B., 15, 34–35, 37–39, 43, 46–47, 56, 62, 65, 67, 70–75, 77, 85, 88

Mercer, Hugh, 77

Missionary Ridge, Battle of, 23, 27, 31, 108

Mississippi, Military Division of the, 23

Narrative of Military Operations, 112

Nashville, Tn., 34, 100

Nashville, Battle of, 111

Natchez, Ms., 116

New Hope Church, 45

New Orleans, La., 116

New York City, NY., 115

Newnan, Ga., 96

Newton, John, 67

Ohio, U.S. Department of the, 23

Olmstead, Charles, 109

O'Neal, Edward, 70

Oostanaula River, 37, 42

Owingsville, Ky., 14

Palmer, John, 67, 98

Palmetto, Ga., 94

Parrot rifles (artillery pieces), 83

Peachtree Creek (and Battle of), 46, 61, 64, 67, 70–75, 84, 86

Peninsular Campaign, 17, 26
Pickett's Mill, Ga., 45
Polk, Leonidas, 37, 42, 43, 61
Preston, Sally (Buck), 18, 20, 70, 115
Preston, William, 70

Quartermaster Department, Army of Tennessee, 63

Red Clay, Tn., 35
Regiments, C.S.:
    1st Georgia Infantry, 109
    4th Texas Infantry, 16, 17
Regiments, U.S.:
    4th Kentucky Mounted Infantry, 94
    123d Illinois Mounted Infantry, 47
    2d U.S. Cavalry, 16, 49
Reilly, John, 98
Resaca, Ga., 37–38, 42–43, 71
Reynolds, Daniel, 70
Richmond, Va., 16–18, 20–21, 23, 26, 28–31, 48–49, 51, 54, 59,
    62, 85, 103, 113, 115
Ringgold, Ga, 35
Rocky Face Ridge, 37
Rough and Ready, Ga., 106–107
Ross, L.S. (Sul), 99, 102

Schofield, John M., 15, 34–35, 37, 43, 56, 62, 65, 67, 74, 82,
    98–99, 106, 111
Scott, Thomas, 69
Seddon, James, 30, 55
Senate, C.S., 20
Seven Days' Battles, 17
Seven Pines, Battle of, 26
Sharp, Jacob, 80–83
Sheridan, Philip H., 15
Sherman, William T., 23–25, 27, 31, 33–34, 37–38, 42–43,
    45–48, 53, 56, 61–62, 64, 67, 69, 71, 74–75, 77, 82, 84–90,
    93–94, 96–100, 102–103, 106–107, 110, 111, 113–115

Shiloh, Battle of, 114
Shoup, Francis, 87
Slocum, Henry, 89, 102, 110
Smith, Edmund Kirby, 16, 49
Smith, Giles, 77
Smith, G.W., 65, 74, 80
Smith, Morgan, 82, 91, 92
Smyrna, Ga., 46
Snake Creek Gap, 35, 37–39
South Carolina, 115
Stanley, David S., 89, 103, 106, 108
Stevens, Clement, 56, 69
Stevenson, Carter, 80
Stewart, Alexander P., 30, 55, 61, 65, 67, 69–71, 74, 80, 91, 93
Stoneman, George, 16, 89, 94, 96, 102
Sweeny, Thomas, 75, 77

Tennessee, 20, 27, 30, 33, 35, 100, 111
Tennessee Campaign, 115
Tennessee, C.S. Department of, 55
Tennessee, U.S. Department of the, 24
Texas, 16, 115–116
Thomas, George H., 16, 33, 35, 37, 43, 61–62, 64–65, 67, 69,
    71–72, 74, 85, 102–103, 106, 111
Trans-Mississippi Department, C.S., 49
Troup House, 80, 82–83
Tunnel Hill, Ga., 35, 37

United States Military Academy (West Point), 14, 15, 17, 34,
    49, 56
Utoy Creek, 98

Van Dorn, Earl, 16
Vaughn, Alfred, 79
Venable, Charles, 17
Vicksburg, Ms., 23, 26, 89
Virginia, 61, 96–97, 114
Virginia Peninsula, 16

Walcutt, Charles, 77
Walker, W.H.T., 69, 75, 88
Walthall, Edward, 70, 93
Ward, William, 67, 69, 70
Washington, D.C., 115
Watkins, Sam, 26, 56, 79
West, Granville, 94, 96
West Point (see United States Military Academy)
Western & Atlantic Railroad, 35, 37, 42, 45, 62, 64, 100, 111
Wheeler, Joseph, 27–28, 30, 37, 65, 67, 73–74, 84, 90, 94, 96,
    99, 100
Wilderness, Battle of, 61, 114
Williams, Alpheus, 67, 70
Wytheville, Va., 114

Yorktown, Va., 16

CPSIA information can be obtained at www.ICGtesting.com
Printed in the USA
LVOW082147130513

333641LV00004B/154/A